THINKING FROM THE EDGE

THINKING FROM THE EDGE

ALAN R. GAWITH

First published in 2006 by
Apex Publishing Ltd
PO Box 7086, Clacton on Sea, Essex, CO15 5WN

www.apexpublishing.co.uk

**British Library Cataloguing-in-Publication Data
A catalogue record for this book
is available from the British Library**

ISBN 1-904444-73-3 978-1-904444-73-2

Typeset in 11pt Times New Roman

Production Manager: Chris Cowlin

Cover Design: Andrew Macey

Printed and bound in Great Britain

DEDICATION

They can't take the blame but they should take some of the credit, since many of my insights and much of the experience out of which this small book arose was experience shared - shared over many years and in so many ways.

So thank you to Kit, and all our family and all their families.

Alan

PREFACE

I was born in 1924 into a Quaker family. Went to a Quaker school, the during the war, served with the Friends' Ambulance Unit in London, Holland and Germany. That background has remained a strong influence upon my life, study and work. Ordained priest in the Church of England 1957; served in a number of different parishes in the north, then became Social Responsibility Officer for Manchester Diocese 1974-1989 and HIV/AIDS Adviser 1988-1992. Hon. Canon of Manchester 1982-1989.

Religion and religious belief, religious institutions and spirituality are very much in the 'public eye' now. They are matters of public concern whether linked to pluralities of ethnic groups, faiths, cultures, histories, or to fears of terrorism, or Faith schools, or the influence of 'moral majorities', etc.

These are also the author's concerns and the book, written for the interested but not for the specialist, focuses upon religious belief and the faults, dangers, manipulations, responsibilities and joys of religious belief.

The title 'Thinking from the Edge' probably reflects my love/hate relationship with the Church, the fact that I am retired after a long and varied ministry, and that I am now an octogenarian. There must be at least three edges there!

It does not pretend to be an academic work. Distinctively, it springs from and reflects the author's conviction that religion should be more about **questions than answers: faith is a questing spirit!**

CONTENTS

PROLOGUE: TWO IMAGES

At one time, the church, with the town hall and market square, must have proclaimed the town centre.
It has always seemed to me a beautiful building, with the warm sandstone, long nave and solid tower. It stands, a long memory of many generations and the passage of time and events.
Especially in the morning sun, the warmth of those sandstone walls glows like an assurance of solidarity with, and affirmation of, all those people whose lives have weaved the warp and woof of the town's history or mined its glories and its tragedies.
"All shall be well and all manner of things shall be well."
In changing times there are still unchanging values.

A day or two after the clocks changed and it was early dusk, I stood at the top of the Avenue and it gripped me suddenly!
I turned back and looked again: I had never seen that before and it was discomforting.
It was no longer the beauty and warmth, solidarity, assurance and affirmation that met me. Instead, the dark, squat tower, the tall, shadowed nave and tower and walls surmounted by castlellated stonework, silhouetted black against the last lights of the sky, clamped down over the town and I shivered.
For the first time the east end of the church powerfully reminded me of a throne - the shape etched stark and dark against the evening sky. Perhaps it still symbolised things temporal and spiritual, but now they were the harsh compacts between State and Church; the millstones between which history and lives were ground.

I guess both images are true.

CHAPTER 1

THINKING FROM THE EDGE

Come to the edge.
No, we will fall ...
They came to the edge.
He pushed them, and they flew.
(from Guillaume Apollinaire)

WHAT ARE THE ROOTS OF CHRISTIAN FAITH?

1) The sense, which seems to be shared by most, if not all, human beings and human communities across the centuries - that **we are made for MORE** and our world is made for more. That MORE is to do with goodness and love, care, justice, joy and responsibility for each other and our world.
That sense may delight us, motivate us, torment us, frighten and tease us. We may acknowledge it, welcome it or flatly deny it - but, for most, it does seem to be there whether we pursue it or are pursued by it.

2) That MORE is the basic religious sense and drive. So we may say that the MORE is God or the energy and the spirit of God. Perhaps this is another way of putting it: it is "the awareness of a depth in an observable world that goes beyond what is observable". (Richard Holloway's phrase I think.)

3) That MORE, for many of us, is partially spelt out, sketched in the Bible. There is a record of human beings in a particular time, place and history, reaching out towards that MORE, with longing and hope, and that MORE, God, reaching down towards human beings, revealing

him/herself, inviting and calling us to walk on his/her WAY.
You must go to Rome sometime and lie on the floor of the Sistine Chapel and gaze at that wonderful scene, painted by Michelangelo, of God creating Adam. God reaches out his right hand, his first finger *almost* touching the first finger of Adam's left hand - giving life to the first human.
That picture is also a wonderful metaphor of what the Bible is about! The reaching down and the reaching up; the *almost* touching - the space between, which leaves room for all sorts of human misunderstanding and misrepresentation, distortion and human arrogance. God and God's truth, beauty and goodness are not always obvious to we humans, and maybe we are not always so keen on them even when we do perceive them! We often feel in the dark - seeing, as it were, 'through a glass, darkly'. So we may often miss, or be blind to, the creative hand of God.

4) But the further reality of God, for Christians, is in the coming of life and complete givenness of Jesus. There God (the MORE) is 'earthed'; God, crystallised out on our Earth, in human circumstance, situation and history.
Whether the language we use is like that or speaks of 'the Son of God' and the Virgin Mary and the wonderful Nativity stories - Jesus is perceived as a metaphor of God.

5) By and through Jesus Christ, through his life, attitudes, teaching, death and Resurrection, God is shown to be in, with, and for the 'whole', not just some part or portion of the Earth, the world and its human beings and its creatures.
God is shown not to be Earth-bound but calling the Earth, the world, to a fuller life, a life marked by goodness and love, care and justice and responsibility for each other and our world.

6) The measure of our relationship and our response to God is there, in the here and now of our relationships on Earth - to each other and

to our world.

7) Our hope and confidence for this 'responsibility' lies in the fact that **we are all, each and every one, made in the image of God**. The Spirit of God is indeed already in us and in our world. Furthermore, it lies in the faith/trust that God is Love and "*that God so loved the world that he gave the Son ... in order that all who have faith in him should not perish*" (in the circle of their own self, self-interest, selfishness) "*but should win eternal life*" (qualitative not quantitative - in and of the quality, the spirit, the way, of Jesus's life).
That God is Love is evidenced for us by the self-givenness of Jesus's life in love, trust, acceptance and search for truth and justice - right up to the end. Read the account of Jesus praying in the Garden of Gethsemane : Mark 14:32-42.

8) Yet the end was not the death of Jesus. The end, the consummation, for Jesus - and for us - is in the Resurrection and the past, present and future under the light of the Resurrection. Through it we are assured of God's continuing Spirit in the world, the Spirit of Jesus still open, welcoming, available to us and for us, the world and the future. With the assurance comes the commission - to work for God's way in the world; the early Christians were known as the 'People of the Way'.
The Resurrection of Jesus Christ in and through the hearts, minds and bodies open to his Spirit brings before us the **immense possibilities of life renewed, transformed** in the Spirit of God.

As Richard Holloway puts it (*'Doubts and Loves' - Canongate 2001*):

If we say we believe in the Resurrection it only has meaning if we are people who believe in the possibility of transformed lives, transformed attitudes and transformed societies. The action is proof of the belief.

Resurrection is the refusal to be imprisoned any longer by history and its long hatreds; it is the determination to take the first step out of the tomb.

TOO, TOO, MANY WORDS!

"Poor little talkative Christianity!" said E. M. Forster.
Here we are, just now, adding to it, and we have done so across the centuries, more perhaps to boost and protect the Christian Institution, the Church, and to maintain order and power, than to grow in faith and be stretched by faith towards the infinite possibilities of renewal in the Spirit of God.
We have spent more time defining, ringing around and setting limits upon 'believing' than we have given quiet time, thought and creative imagination to faith and faithfulness.
When the sixth-form girls from Kendal High School pointedly sat down and read their books as the Creed was recited in the Service or stood up with firmly closed mouths, they were making an honest statement and the Church had in fact sold them short in the currency of God!
Christianity, Christian discipleship, is not about beliefs; faith is not about beliefs. It is about relationship, and trust. The relationship with God and the relationship with people and with the world is indivisible. God as Creator (and that really has nothing to do with literal understandings of the creation stories in the book of Genesis, nor with Intelligent Design!) and the great commandment - *to love the Lord your God with all your being and to love your neighbour as yourself*, make that abundantly clear.
We need to be reminded that that mysterious, haunting MORE is still there whether we are talking about evolution and the future of humanity, or beyond humanity, and about the beginning and the end of the universe or whether we are talking about religion, about the Bible or different faiths, different people and the sheer multiplicity of differences that inhabit, confuse and invigorate our world.
Indeed Rabbi Jonathan Sacks maintains that the heart of monotheism is that **unity creates diversity**:

The glory of the created world is its astonishing multiplicity... if we listen carefully, we will hear the voice of God telling us something we need to know ...We will make peace only when we learn that God loves difference and so, at last, must we. God has created many cultures, civilisations and faiths but only one world in which to live together - it is getting smaller all the time.

We human beings do not determine the limits to nature's development or to God's grace and kingdom or way. As an ancient Jewish teaching puts it:

When a human being makes many coins in the same mint, they all come out the same. God makes every person in the same image - His image - and each is different.
(Jonathan Sacks, The Dignity of Difference.)

Besides the 'astonishing multiplicity', there are also the vast 'unknowns', huge and minuscule. Scientists are often better at acknowledging that and doing so with humility than are many people who address those realities from a distinctly 'religious' standpoint.
The words of an old nobleman from the court of King Edwin of Northumbria, we should hear. He spoke after Bishop Paulinus had pleaded the case for Christianity:

The present life on earth, O King, as compared with the whole length of time, which is unknowable to us, seems to me to be like this: as if, when you are sitting at dinner with your chiefs and ministers in wintertime ... One of the sparrows from outside flew very quickly through the hall, as if it came in one door and soon went through another. In that actual time it is indoors it is not touched by winter's storm; but yet the tiny period of calm is over in a moment, and having come out of the winter it soon returns to the winter and slips out of your sight. Man's life appears to be more or less like this, and of what my follow it, or what preceded

it, we are absolutely ignorant.
(From Bede's Ecclesiastical History, quoted by Richard Holloway in Doubts & Loves.)

The temptation is to close down on the MORE, to limit God to a clear, acceptable vision upon which we may focus and to which we may commit ourselves. Sadly, we do often impose our own limits and exploitations, our own exclusions and condemnations - in God's name - upon the world that he has gifted to us, the world he has entrusted to us. An horrific and immediate example of that is in a newspaper of 11 October 2005: "Most of those now seeking to blow people up - whether with tanks and missiles or rucksacks and passenger planes - do so in the name of God". If that is at all true, we have to ask what is it about religion that enables it to be used to apparently 'legitimate' such action, and to motivate or fire up individuals to 'sacrifice' their own lives in that horrific cause?

Closing down on the MORE may have something to do with that; it may enable some people to have such a narrowed view of God that what would naturally be regarded as 'evil' could be called 'good'. It would by no means be the first time in the history of religion. But that closing down is more clearly shown, and chosen because, although there may be other important and wider visions in our complex, plural, fractured and threatened world, **the most important need is felt to be to focus upon one thing, and that is the perfection of the self**.

Some may think that is just a selfish vanity, but there are many others for whom it is a serious priority because that is the path of repentance from sin, and salvation through God's sacrifice of his Son, and justification through faith, that may bring them into the freedom of the sons (and daughters) of God and the assurance of heavenly life after death.

Perhaps that accounts, at least in part, for the rise in the Christian Church of literalist approaches to scripture and more personal and absolutist approaches to doctrine and Christian practice. This type of single-minded focus and vision is certainly biblical, but are there not

also biblical grounds for, and a need for, a more uncertain, adventurous, open, partial and vulnerable approach?
Those two approaches have been called the 'hedgehog' and the 'fox' concepts of Christian faith and life:

The hedgehog relates everything to a single vision, whereas the fox pursues many ends, often unrelated and even contradictory. The hedgehog operates in a centripetal way, drawing things into the circle, whereas the fox is centrifugal, flinging out in all directions. (Isaiah Berlin, quoted by Dr Stephen Cherry)

Jonathan Sacks suggests that the hedgehog is the 'saint' whereas the fox is the 'sage': the saint focuses on the perfection of the self; the sage focuses on the perfection of society.

Stephen Cheery remarks: As a consequence, the sage develops social virtues such as justice, fairness, integrity, patience, a love of peace, an ability to hear both sides of an argument and weigh conflicting situations.

It is extremely difficult, under all the pressures of a functional, fragmented and factionalised world, for foxes to thrive. All the pressure is to identify a 'hedgehog concept or vision', and focus on it.

But it simply will not do to curl up into a prickly ball! No doubt we need both hedgehogs and foxes, but Stephen Cherry rightly suggests that the grander challenge is to be a fox, "for it leads not to certainty, comfort or clarity; rather, it is the way of trust, trial, and transformation." It is perhaps the only way of opening up a wonderful, liberating, exciting and challenging faith that may really get alongside the deepest longings, hopes, energies and joys of men, women and children and their multiplicity of differences.
(For the above thoughts I am indebted to Dr Stephen Cherry's article in the *Church Times*, 07.10.05.)

SOME CLOSING DOWN WE MUST OPEN UP

THE BIBLE: THE BOREDOM AND THE TINGLE FACTOR

It's odd isn't it that, at a time when probably most people find the Bible boring and irrelevant, a larger section of Church people than was the case in the past now believe it literally and uncritically. That, of course, leads to more people rejecting the Bible as nonsense, and often as cruel and irrational nonsense at that.
Some years ago Dr Jeffrey John wrote in an article called *'The Bible and Homosexuality'* (Christian Action Journal, 1990):

> *Most Christians still approach the Bible with essentially fundamentalist presuppositions ... With a deep-seated instinct that the Bible is to be unquestioningly revered as the direct source of God's will and word ... a single source of literal, inerrant truth ....*

Certainly, for many, that is still the case. But why, when so many Christians reject the claim of the Roman Catholic Church of the 'literal, inerrant truth of the Pope' when speaking, *ex cathedra*, on matters of faith and morals, do they happily claim the Bible as a 'single source of literal, inerrant truth'? Especially when in much of the Bible, particularly in the New Testament, people, individuals and communities are being called to become the 'locus' of the Spirit of God and to become fellow builders, with God, of the kingdom, the way, of God!
The book, or rather the books, of the Bible are very important. But that library is a very varied collection, arising at different times and from many different authors and out of many differing cultures and with many different editors. The canon of the writings that make up our Bible was itself determined by the Church authorities and involved the exclusion of other writings and was obviously influenced by the situation and interest of the Church at the time. Then, of course, there were various translations and there was the very powerful influence of

'ownership' of the Bible: who transmitted and interpreted the Bible to the mass of people who were illiterate - and, of course, before printing had been invented? The Bible was in the hands of the Church and, in particular, of the monks, nuns and clergy: they were the transmitters and interpreters. When English versions of the Bible came along and printing gave ordinary people access to the written word, the Church and clergy could no longer remain the 'gatekeepers' of the Bible. As Archbishop Michael Ramsay wrote:

> *It is to men and women not 'in vacuo' but in the contemporary content of their existence that the Word in the Bible speaks, ... the faith of a Christian is faith in God, and God is the giver of the scholar's quest for truth as he sets out in search of it, as one not knowing whither he goes (The Authority of the Bible', Peake's Commentary, 1962).*

We need now more then ever to hear Michael Ramsay's words:

> *It would be wrong to infer from the exalted place of the Bible in every form of Christianity that Christianity is the religion of a Book. The central fact of Christianity is not a Book but a Person - Jesus Christ, himself described as the Word of God.*

There are many 'tingle points' - and not only in the New Testament. Spot them in the following reflection on what the Bible is about:

* IT IS ABOUT a people who have lost their way, and the social symptoms of that loss are seen in violence, disorder and chaos, in greed, arrogance, exploitation, hunger, thirst - the physical and spiritual wilderness experience - and despair.

* A people who from time to time realise their loss or are called by far-sighted critics and dissenters to recognise and repent of that loss - for it is largely a matter of choice.

* A people who, out of the depth of their loss, long for, search for and reach out towards hope, hope beyond the horizon, the new world, new possibilities.

* A people struggling towards the light, the life, the promise that they feel is in their innermost being.

* A people who sometimes know the experience of 'God with them', who are breathless with excitement, filled with awe at the greatness and wonder of God.

* A people upon whom, now and again, God explodes in an electric storm of enlightenment and insight.

* A people who are well aware of the human drama that is the context of their lives - personal, tribal and national.

* A people who are continually teased by the conviction that the human drama is itself part of a divine drama - 'God, in whom we live and move and have our being'.

So there is philosophy here, there is politics here, there is morality here, there is emotion, idealism and certainly humanity here. What this amounts to is 'literature', all sorts of literature, much of it inspired 'literature' - but probably not much real history.

(For much of that thinking I am indebted to Thomas L. Thompson's *The Bible in History - How Writers Create a Past.*)

Here are some tingle points from St John's Gospel:

In the beginning the Word was.
And the Word was with God,
And the Word was God ...

And the Word became flesh
And pitched his tent among us,
Full of grace and truth.
(from John's Prologue)

For God so loved the world that he gave his only Son,
That whoever believes in him should not perish but have eternal life.
(Jn 3:16)

This record has been made
so that you may believe
that Jesus is the Christ,
The Son of God,
and that, believing,
you may have life eternal in his Being.
(Jn 20:31)

And one from St Luke:

Jesus came to the synagogue at Nazareth
and read aloud from the prophet Isaiah -
The Spirit of the Lord is upon me,
because he has anointed me
to bring good news to the poor.
He has sent me
to proclaim release to the captive
and recovery of sight to the blind,
to let the oppressed go free,
to proclaim the year of the Lord's favour,
- then he rolled up the scroll
and gave it back to the attendant.
He then said:
today this scripture has been fulfilled in your hearing.
(Lk 4:16-21)

The best commentary upon those passages, and many others, might be the story of the two caterpillars! There were two caterpillars lying on a beach watching a butterfly going by. One caterpillar nudged the other and said, "You'd never catch me going up in one of those things!"
Go on - read the Bible and search out till you find some of those tingle points where you do really feel a mixture perhaps of: 'you'd never catch me going up in one of those things' and 'if only I could - let's try!'

GADZOOKS!

Maybe the Jews were wise, and the Buddhists, for neither had a word for God. Or perhaps the Jews had a word but would not use it because God could not be comprehended in a word.
Too often it has become a word - a word for the incomprehensible - that we hook into and then too often pretend that we have hooked the reality: God is caught, displayed, on the pages of the Church or the determination of our minds. But that cannot be so, or, at most, it can be only partial and transient.
"But now you will ask me, 'How am I to think of God himself, and what is he?' and I cannot answer you except to say, 'I do not know!' For with this question you have brought me into the same darkness, the same cloud of unknowing where I want you to be. For though we, through the grace of God, can know fully about all other matters, and think about them - yes, even the very works of God himself - yet of God himself can no man think". Then the unknown author of *The Cloud of Unknowing* continues: "Therefore I will leave on one side everything I can think, and choose for my love that thing which I cannot think! Why? Because he may well be loved, but not thought."
'Manzooks' would have been a more accurate title than 'Gadzooks', for it is not God who gets his hooks into man, but man - mankind - that tries so hard to tie God down, to overdefine God in order to fit

him/her/it into our 'requirements', our preconceptions; in order to 'control'.
The Church's doctrine of the Holy Trinity - Father, Son and Holy Spirit, three Persons and one God - is seen by many as a gross and meaningless over-definition. It is a doctrine that teases many, infuriates some and delights others, probably in spite of its history and intention. Delights - because it can be seen as an inspired affirmation both of the indefinability of God and of the multiplicity and wonderful variation of the wholeness of the one God. It shows us how God will stretch us - always stretch our minds and hearts - and how stretching out towards one part, element, Person, of that God-reality is to touch upon the whole reality. It is an encouragement to grow, to stretch and to know that we can never 'contain' the whole - thank God!
But that must also mean that we trod dangerously, on uncertain ground, when we wrote in the first section - 'The Roots of the Faith' - about the MORE and God. We were seeing the MORE, in human minds, as a metaphor for GOD - nothing wrong with that. We were perceiving the MORE through Christian spectacles - nothing wrong with that providing we recognise that it is 'through Christian spectacles' and not a factual account and therefore not a factual 'certainty'.
It is just that 'pretended certainty' that does harm. If we could but accept that religion is not about certainty - there are very few, if any, certainties, and those that do exist are either 'faith certainties', not factual, like the faith that God really is, or we may be speaking of, for example, the certainty that Jesus lived. Although that is an incontrovertible fact, it does only tell us that Jesus lived. For the meaning and significance of Jesus and his life and teaching we do not have that factual certainty. Instead, we are called to faith responses to what we may perceive in our deepest being - in that of God within us, that MORE that resonates within us - as a faith, trust, relationship certainty: something to search into, something to expand and stretch us and our humanity.
Perhaps it can help us, give us more confidence, when we see the

resonances between Jesus and Mohammed. Jelaluddin Rumi, a thirteenth-century Sufi, poet and founder of the 'Whirling Dervishes' wrote this:

The mystery of spiritual emptiness
May be living in a pilgrim's heart, and yet
The knowing of it may not yet be his.

Wait for the illuminating openness,
As though your chest was filling with light,
As when God said,
'Did We not expand you'? (Qur'an 94:1)

Don't look for it outside yourself.
You are the source of milk. Don't milk others!

There is a milk fountain inside you.
Don't walk around with an empty bucket.

You have a channel into the ocean, and yet
You ask for water from a little pool.

Beg for that love expansion. Meditate only
On THAT. The Qur'an says,
'And He is with you' (57:4)

(From *The Essential Rumi*, translated by Coleman Barks, Castle Books, 1997)

Certainty is the common arrogance of both bad science and bad religion. In both cases it is tempting because it plays into human desires and hungers for security and human needs for healing and assurance.

That sense of the MORE to which we have referred may be arrived at in different ways. Robert Winston has remarked that some studies from biology, psychology and neuroscience do suggest that religious ideas and behaviour have evolved perhaps out of a sense of need. David Sloan Wilson. in his book *Darwin's Cathedral*, says that religiosity emerged as a 'useful' genetic trait because it had the effect of making social groups more unified. The communal nature of religion would have given groups of hunter-gatherers a stronger sense of togetherness. The better the religion was at producing an organised and disciplined group, the more effective they would have been at staying alive, and hence at passing their genes on to the next generation. That may suggest that ideas and codes of morality, of relationships and personal and interpersonal behaviour, are developed and transmitted socially and genetically. Religion, or at least religious behaviour, might therefore be seen as part of the process of 'natural selection'.

As Robert Winston notes:

> *Religion does not seem to be produced by a specific part of our psychological make-up. ... Is it more likely, then, that religious ideas are something of an accidental by-product created by other parts of our basic blueprint, by processes deep in the unconscious mind that evolved to help us survive?*

But for eminent sociologist Emile Durkheim (1858-1917), according to Wilson in *Darwin's Cathedral*, the by-product theories of religious ideas and belief were inadequate because, for him, "religious belief is abandoned when it fails to have secular utility". He explained religion as fundamentally functional for its members. Wilson claims that a new approach to understanding functionalism in relation to religion now comes about through progress in evolutionary biology together with the unification of the human social sciences.

The argument from design as evidence for the existence of God comes up in renewed forms now as 'Intelligent Design'. Theologian William Paley (1743-1805), in the early part of the nineteenth century, popularised the argument from design in his book *National Theology*.

But in fact, writes Wilson, "it only provides evidence for a designing agent - the hand of God, a human engineer, alien visitors from another planet, or the process of natural selection!"
However, one thing is certain and that is that religion is as much a part of human self-understanding and expression as ever. It is not a time for the churches and other religious institutions to bemoan their fate or to be depressed or to give up - and certainly not to curl up into a tight ball like a hedgehog! Nor is it a time simply to dig in our heels and defy the open and honest search of modern knowledge into our histories, scriptures, doctrines and dogmas, and how we use them. Faith, doubt, trust, exploration and relationship can all go together, and together free us from the shackles and idolatries of the comfortable captivity that is sometimes religion.

A MORE IMAGINATIVE 'CREDO'

IN GOD, towards whom, or what, people have ever reached out longingly, fearfully, urgently, crying out from the depths of their spirits: 'We are made for more, and our world is made for more!'

IN GOD, who as in the Sistine Chapel, reaches down towards humanity, giving, creating, wanting to be known, to be received.

IN GOD, whose index finger almost touched Adam, thus allowing the space for misunderstanding, misrepresentation and all sorts of accidental and deliberate confusions. IN GOD who is revealed, disguised and hidden before us through many scriptures.

IN GOD, whose world, whose universe, this somehow is, and whose energy, beauty, life and order are reflected there and are felt, seen, enjoyed and exploited by us.

IN GOD, who, somehow, is that MORE towards which, time and

again, we know we are called - by our very being and, sometimes, in spite of ourselves.

IN GOD, who perhaps even through evolution, through the evolving consciousness of human beings, leads us to the attractive possibility of goodness, of kindness, of altruism.

IN GOD, in whom indeed, "we live and move and have our being" - but often have not the eyes to see nor the ears to hear, and our ignorance is proved upon the backs of the poor and marginalised people of the world.

IN GOD, in whose image each and every human being is created - whatever colour, nationality, history, culture, sexual orientation, disability or religion - and called, through 'difference', to new life and possibilities.

IN GOD, who comes down to us, into our own personal drama of good and evil; into the responsibilities and possibilities, the joys and sadnesses, the gifts and losses, that life brings to us: "The Word became flesh."

IN GOD, who draws us towards "the still point of the turning world. … at the still point, there the dance is." IN GOD, who draws us through the faith/trust inspired wonderfully in Jesus Christ and given to us in the 'earthing' of God among us, in the crystallising-out of Goodness on earth in the person, life and love of Jesus Christ.

IN GOD, who is, who would be, the God of Relationship, who reveals that through those who respond in faith/trust, a relationship of love, care, compassion, given fully - 'even to death on a cross'. A relationship that for us, through the Resurrection of Jesus Christ, calls us across all barriers, all frontiers, all disappointments and deaths with the promise of forgiveness and renewal and all the nurturing and exciting possibilities of the Kingdom of God, the Way, the Spirit of God in and for the world.

IN GOD, the same God, who has shown him/herself in many other ways to other people and would call us to affirm with them, 'the dignity of difference'.

IN GOD, the same God, who with them, as with us, respects human freedom, giving space for 'misunderstandings, misrepresentations and all sorts of accidental and deliberate confusions'.

IN GOD, whose first "Yes!' is to the world - and yet we all too frequently use his/her name mistakenly and fruitlessly, to escape the world. The world is God's agenda and we are to make it our agenda: perhaps that is God's Human Project, through Jesus Christ - to make the world our agenda, the world as it is and the world as it could be, as it could become ... That becoming calls and challenges all of us, each person, community, institution, profession, trade, industry, state and nation, in the name of Love, Justice, Trust, Generosity and Co-operation.

IN GOD, who is not greatly sold on 'beliefs'!

You have been told, man, what is good!
He requires only one thing from you:
do justice and be there for others,
match God in your life.
(Micah 6:6,7. Dorothee Sölle's translation in *Thinking About God*)

THE MESSAGE OF EASTER

JESUS CHRIST IS THE LAMB OF GOD, IN WHOM IS LIFE

That is the message of Easter; that is the principal and most urgent message of Christianity.
It is a here and now, and becoming message.
It is a godly/human message, a transcendence-in-the-midst message.
So let us look at Easter - without which there would be no Church, no Gospels, no New Testament, no Sunday, no Eucharist or Holy Communion - no Christianity at all.
That also must mean that Easter is not just the major Festival in the Church's calendar; not just a once-a-year celebration, lambs springing and eggs a'rolling.
It is not just Sunday but every day, and the message every day and to all and each of us is - the message of Easter is:

LIFE IS FOR LIVING AND LIFE IS FOR LOVING

True, we cannot separate Easter from Good Friday, the Resurrection from the Crucifixion, any more than we can separate good from evil in the world, or the presence of joy from the presence of pain and suffering in our world.
But the way that the Christian message of Easter has often been transmitted, through the language it has used, makes a travesty of the truth.
Let's explore that a little through the medium of an Easter sermon, Easter Day 2005:

Now the green blade riseth from the buried grain,
Wheat that in dark earth many days has lain;
Love lives again, that with the dead has been:
Love is come again,
Like wheat that springeth green.

Forth he came at Easter, like the risen grain,
He that for three days in the grave had lain,
Quick from the dead my risen Lord is seen:

When our hearts are wintry, grieving, or in pain,
Thy touch can call us back to life again,
Fields of our hearts that dead and bare have been;
Love is come again,
Like wheat that springeth green.

A universal, powerful, hopeful image of EASTER and its meaning! And that I suppose is perhaps where the chickens and bunnies fit in - but with some difficulty because they miss out 'the winter'! Easter eggs, delicious as they are, have the same problem very often.
Easter can be a quietly great time for children, young people and adults if we take time to consider and communicate its personal and universal, deeper and richer meaning.
At the back of that meaning is something horrific, violent and shameful.
Stanley Spencer, a painter who believed that "Love is the essential power in the creation of art" yet painted a Crucifixion, set, as many of his religious paintings, in his village of Cookham in Berkshire - a Crucifixion that was stark and uncompromising in the human cruelty depicted. It prompted the Bishop of Oxford to write:

This is a disturbing painting. But the Crucifixion of Christ, like all expressions of human cruelty, is rightly disturbing ... The reality was as painful a form of torture as human ingenuity has devised. And this, sadly, is what human beings are still capable of.
(Church Times, 18.03.05)

Yet still many hymns and many sermons speak of God's wrath, God's vengeance towards sinful humanity, sinful human beings. A wrath, a vengeance, that can only be assuaged or satisfied by severe, cruel punishment - only, in fact, by a blood sacrifice - the sacrifice of God's Son, of Jesus.

There was no other good enough
To pay the price of sin;
He only could unlock the gate
Of heaven, and let us in.

He died that we might be forgiven
He died to make us good,
That we might go at last to heaven,
Saved by his precious blood.

So salvation is ours through that complex, cruel, bloody sacrifice - as in the film, *The Passion of Christ.* BUT is that picture of God (the Father) really the picture of the God you believe in?

Not long ago, in response to the truly remarkable love and commitment of Gemma, Donna, Cath and Paula, the sisters of Robert McCartney, and Bridgeen, his fiancée, the IRA offered to shoot those who had murdered Robert McCartney. Their philosophy seemed to be: to prove that we care, we are prepared to murder our brave volunteers - a crime to cancel out a crime; killing will be exonerated by more killing! As Dr Giles Fraser suggested, that sketches a sort of "moral universe uncomfortably close to much of the theology that we have often been asked to take on board in Holy Week."

But that sort of moral universe is a long way from Jesus. Jesus's theology, his understanding of God, was almost the opposite of that: his was a proclamation of human freedom, of human liberation and possibility, as people made in the image of God, who had the kingdom of God 'within them'. "Salvation is then about being unconditionally released from a mountain of obligation."

Look at the way Jesus responds to Mary Magdalene on that first Easter Day - Mary Magdalene, who was said to have been possessed by seven devils (Luke Ch. 8) and to have been a repentant prostitute

(Luke Ch. 7). No! Here is tremendous, quiet assurance - for now and for the future: "Jesus said to her, 'Mary'! She turned, and said to him in Hebrew, 'Rabbouni'! which means teacher."
True, for that assurance, for those blossoming possibilities, there is a condition - which is part of the Lord's Prayer: forgive us our sins, as we forgive those who sin against us! And if, as the Baptist minister, the Revd Steve Chalke asked, "IF we are saved by Jesus's death on the cross, why did he need to rise again?"
But Easter is the greatest Festival of the Christian Church and the Christian year. The Resurrection is the climax of the Gospels; without the Resurrection the Gospels would never have been written!
The universal, powerful, hopeful image of Easter and the Resurrection is in much more than the glorious Spring of nature. The poet E. E. Cummings stretches towards that in this odd but lovely poem:

I thank YOU God for most this amazing
Day: for the leaping greenly spirits of trees
and a blue true dream of sky; and for everything
which is natural which is infinite which is yes

(I who have died am alive again today,
and this is the sun's birthday; this is the birth
day of life and of love and wings: and of the gay
great happening illimitably earth)

how should tasting touching hearing seeing
breathing any - lifted from the no
of all nothing - human merely being
doubt unimaginable YOU?

(now the ears of my ears awake and
now the eyes of my eyes are opened)

(Selected Poems, 1923-1958 - Faber)

Just as the cruelty and violence and horror of the Crucifixion are picked up and repeated across the world and across the centuries, less easy sometimes to see but there nevertheless are the images of the Resurrection, in countless examples of human gentleness and joy and supreme effort for goodness, truth and love - and often in hard, forbidding circumstances. And often also in very simple and sometimes heroically simple ways, like the true stories in Mary Doria Russell's book, *A Thread of Grace*. In 1943, a remnant of the French Jews climb across the Maritime Alps, shepherded by Italian soldiers, returning to their homeland as Italy has broken with Nazi Germany and surrendered to the Allies. They move into a territory of goodness and hospitality, to be sheltered under German persecution by a community in whom, as Russell writes, "goodness was banal", for the saying was current, "If you can help, you must help." Russell continues, "a generosity of spirit hard enough to credit to occasional individuals - but for a whole community ...!"
Is there not a hint of the Resurrection, and what it means for us, in the choices that life presents us with as we mourn the death of someone we love? We can remember them by choosing to keep alive in our own lives what was true and good and beautiful and loving about that life.

Perhaps that is part of, or may be part of, what Richard Holloway speaks of as the 'effectual Resurrection', as distinct from the originating event. Holloway's image is imaginative and exciting:

> *THE RESURRECTION IS LIKE THE BIG BANG, which scientists hypothesise as the originating event in the life of the universe; it is not available to us except by guesswork and theory. Just as scientists engage in reading the effect that is the universe back to its unimaginable moment of its beginning, so theologians have read back from the effects on the disciples to a hypothesis to what caused them.*
> *... [There are] in a sense, two Resurrections: there is the BIG BANG that ignited the Christian movement - the originating event,*

which we can only really guess at. The second is the effectual Resurrection. Which is the continuing impact of Jesus upon history and upon people. The people who had deserted Jesus in fear and fled from his dying, somewhere found the courage to proclaim the meaning of his life; and that transformation, that turnabout, is what we mean by Resurrection.
... If we say we believe in the Resurrection it only has meaning if we are people who believe in the possibility of transformed lives, transformed attitudes and transformed societies. The action is the proof of the belief.
(Richard Holloway, Doubts and Loves - Canongate, 2001)

But it is not just human commitment and effort, for behind and within that must be the release, the confidence that the Big Bang of the Resurrection is now 'instinct' within our world. As Gerard Manley Hopkins wrote:

The world is charged with the grandeur of God.
It will flame out, like shining from shook foil; ...

... And though the last light off the black West went
Oh, morning, at the brown brink eastward, springs -
Because the Holy Ghost over the bent
World broods with warm breath and with "ah!" Bright wings.
(God's Grandeur, Selection of Poems and Prose,
W. H. Gardner, 1953)

So, encouraged, we can perhaps dare to say that this is Easter: the real Christian salvation story (or at least, a very important part of it) lies in the little bands or tags that many, many people are getting and wearing, from Christian Aid, Oxfam, CAFOD, etc. - 'MAKE POVERTY HISTORY'! And in the news that the Commission for Africa is calling on rich countries to write off all their Third World debts.

As Giles Fraser remarked, "That really would be Good News for the poor and freedom for the captive."
End of Sermon! (All Giles Fraser quotes are from his weekly column in the Guardian)

BUT EASTER IS JUST THE BEGINNING

A beginning that is continually remembered, continually proclaimed and acted out in the theatre of the Church - that's what the Eucharist, the Mass, the Holy Communion, the Liturgy are about. It is a great 'pageant of beginning' and, for each and every one, a 'beginning again', caught up in that first originating 'beginning' of Creation and all the givenness of life and its possibilities; reminded of that great givenness in the words: *God so loved the world, that he gave his Son* … .
The givenness of that revealing love, revealing life - another 'beginning' for the world; one that disclosed a new 'beginning' for human-'being', a new beginning, a new purpose for people 'made in the image of God'. A new beginning confirmed - astoundedly confirmed - by the Big Bang, the Resurrection!
A pageant (to quote the dictionary) "arranged for effect" - the 'effectual Resurrection', the impact of the life and energy and love of Jesus upon our lives and the life of the world.
The Eucharist can be for us an adventure into God and the meaning of God for our world - moreover, in the words of Keith Ward, into the meaning of "God's evolutionary cosmos". The Eucharist is therefore an adventure into Love - compassion, justice, care responsibility, joy.
This pageant is central to our Christian life, to our human lives - because Easter is, with its message of liberation to new life and possibilities in God, in that MORE that teases and sketches in our hearts and minds a purpose, a calling, a call through the mists that echoes for us Jesus's Mission Statement, which he made at the very start of his public ministry. In the synagogue at Nazareth he opened the

book of Isaiah and read, "The Spirit of the Lord is upon me because he has anointed me to preach good news to the poor, to proclaim release to the captives and to set at liberty those who are oppressed." (Luke 4.18)
There is a pattern to that pageant that builds up towards the meaning of that climax in the receiving of Holy Communion:

* Perhaps the first shape in the pattern may be best expressed by some words of Jean-Francois Six: "To pray is to sing: not a song of our littleness, but rather a song of God's greatness, as we look on him with love, contemplating him in silence." (Prayer and Hope - Collins, 1971)
* The second is acknowledgement of our falling short of the Glory of God and the assurance of God's forgiveness and acceptance of us.
* The third is the reminder of the MORE and the calling of God and of our need to listen.
* The fourth shape in the pattern is the wonder of God the Creator, the Giver - and thus also the awareness of our sharing in Original Blessing.
* The fifth is the awareness of God's invitation to us, through the life of Jesus Christ, to partake of that life and to follow that way.
* The sixth is, under the metaphor of bread and wine, to be open to, and to receive, that life, that RISEN life - and that 'commission'.
The final shape in the pattern is given in the words spoken at the conclusion of Holy Communion: "Send us out in the power of your Spirit to live and work to your praise and glory" - providing, of course, that we realise that "to your praise and glory" takes us straight into the search for, and the discovery of and the creating or enabling of, that praise and glory in our world, in 'God's evolutionary cosmos'. Translate that into the down-to-earth language of the values we espouse and the choices we make at all levels of life and relationship. As former Archbishop, Michael Ramsay wrote, "The Eucharist is the supreme way in which the people of Christ are, through our great high priest, with God with the world around on their hearts."
Importantly, he writes of the priest celebrant: You will find yourself,

as celebrant at the Eucharist, privileged with a unique intensity to 'be with God with the people on your heart'. Do not therefore approach this act without quiet recollection before, and follow it always with quiet recollection after."

There is no cheap grace about the Eucharist or Holy Communion! But there is a 'discipline' if we are to avoid reducing it to an impression of 'cheap grace'.

This great Easter pageant - for it is always that - is a Resurrection pageant and a time of healing; of healing to troubled, confused and sick minds, bodies and spirits - a time of healing that may be very present personally for some people in that community of worshippers and for some with whom, through concern and prayer, they are connected. But that Resurrection healing energy may also stretch way beyond that hour and place of worship, and we may be among the carriers of that energy - even for the healing of the nations!

The sacrament of Holy Communion is incredibly important and meaningful to so many Christians, yet not to all. But some for whom the sacrament is not vital or important believe strongly - as do members of the Society of Friends - in the sacramental life, and that surely is the purpose of Holy Communion for those to whom that sacrament is important.

Perhaps, whether we ponder the sacrament of Holy Communion or the sacramental life, we might usefully think on these things:

* *Heaven is the circumference of things created, both visible and invisible* (Jon Damascene)
* *It is not as a philosopher, but as Prometheus, that we worship the Christ, - the Man who came down from heaven to give men (men, women, children) the Divine fire* (Burkitt)
* *The eternal in the New Testament is not an uncharacterised duration - it is a Christ-filled magnitude* (Alan Richardson)
* *It is easy, said Marx, to be a saint if you have no wish to 'be human'. But did Marx think it easy to be a human without being a saint?* (Jaques Maritain)

But think 'poetically' not literally!

RELIGIOUS CREDIBILITY DOES NOT LIE IN SCIENTIFIC EVIDENCE!

Except that science will sometimes and correctly prick the pretentious bubbles of religious claims to fact and truth and bring them down to 'earth' - the earth of human imagination and need - and 'stretch' our minds towards the MORE, the transcendent possibilities for life.
Gilbert Markus ('Face to Faith', *Guardian*, 24.1.06) reminds us that in the fifth or sixth century, Pseudo-Dionysius taught that *God is beyond every assertion and every denial.* That may sound like a very useful get-out clause, but no, it is surely a truism because, although religion may be for the most part 'man-made' - and the 'man' significance should not be lost on us! - the drawing, teasing, challenging reality of what we call 'God' is not made by us, not man-made, but is given to us, a gift within human life, human awareness, human unease and human joy. Markus quotes Meister Eckhart, that great Dominican theologian and mystic: *God does not lack being, but wholly transcends it.*
Difficult language indeed, but it does mean, for example, that, as Markus points out, *'God' can never be the answer to any scientific question of causality.*
Perhaps religious credibility, especially in this present age and in Britain, lies less in the traditional religious observance of the institutional Church than in the recognition and affirmation of that human stretch towards that awareness of the transcendent, which goes beyond being - and by that hints at a new or renewed 'human being' with greater responsibilities and possibilities for the 'becoming' world.
To discover this we need to listen to many younger people who are looking for, celebrating and trying to bring about a greater awareness of, and attention to, the environment in which we humans live: an environment that includes all the pluralities of our world of people and

their histories, races, cultures, faiths, gender and sexualities, etc.; an environment, a home, that includes all life, all the richness of life and resources for life with which this earth is blessed. What we do about this: that we have a clear responsibility to care for and nurture, protect and preserve this plurality of life, this home - that is a priority that many young people today rightly urge upon us.

The Church needs to engage more fully and openly with that and with a lively commitment of love, joy and hope. But, unfortunately, the Church exhibits a self-regarding, anxious and fearful concern for its own unity, for its own 'purity' - as some seem to justify the stand against the ordination of women, and now the opposition to women bishops, and the ambivalence about sexuality and gay men. That, together with the greater 'literalist' approach to scripture, too often seem to portray the Christian Church as a backward-reflecting body that does not - dare not - take risks for the Easter Christ in a changing world.

However, for that - for the lively 'becoming' Church in this changing world, able and willing to take the risks for the Easter Christ in the world - the individually perceived 'transcendence' is not enough. We are people; human 'being' finds its meaning in relationship, in society, and that meaning is expressed in myths and rituals that are important: they convey and reinforce meaning.

Therefore the long traditions of religious observance in the worship of the Church are of fundamental importance in the public presentation and commitment of meaning and action.

TAKE ME TO YOUR GOD!

Many nations shall come and say:
"Come, let us go up to the mountain of the Lord,
to the house of the God of Jacob;
that he may teach us his ways

and we may walk in his paths".
(Micah 4:1.2a)

NOT, 'Teach me your religion', because religion is man-made and institutionalised and inevitably, through the mills of history and human fallibility, has become a medium of power and control.

That problem is at the root of religious education and Faith and Church schools as it is at the root of the Prayer for Christian Unity. Religion is not faith. 'Take me to your God' can be a genuine search and request for a faith-relationship that is distinct from any structured religion. Perhaps we can illustrate that by looking at, firstly, the Week of Prayer for Christian Unity, and secondly, at the question of Faith Schools.

THE WEEK OF PRAYER FOR CHRISTIAN UNITY

The Week of Prayer for Christian Unity for 2006 came from Ireland. So perhaps we should ponder the issues, the questions, the needs, from within the context of Northern Ireland.
Seventeen years ago, children came on holiday to Kendal from Belfast: half from the Shankhill, half from the Falls - so half were Catholic, half were Protestant.
Once they had met and spoken, shared dormitories and enjoyed each other, they had a marvellous holiday. But on the coach together, on the way to the boat and the return to Belfast, the children with their new friends were upset because, as they said tearfully, once off the boat at Belfast, they would never be able to meet again.

Thirty-seven years later, on 21 December 2005, this letter appeared in the *Guardian*:

Your leader (December 19th) rightly concludes that 'the overriding objective in Northern Ireland is to build the politics of the future'. It's not the only way of doing this but we could make a start by educating our children here together by seeking to make an integrated school choice for all parents a reality so we can build a shared future....

Eric James suggests:

Whatever leads us to a more profound understanding of each other - across the barriers of race and religion - must surely be of God.

(Collected Thoughts - Continuum, 2002)

Jonathan Sacks reminds us that:

We will make peace only when we learn that God loves difference and so, at last, must we. God has created many cultures, civilisations and faiths but only one world in which to live together - and it is getting smaller all the time.

(The Dignity of Difference, Continuum, 2002)

A Christian Guru, Swami Abhishiktananda, asks:

Who is a Christian? Who is a Hindu? Who is a Muslim? I know only children of my Father who is in heaven. It is not Baptism, neither is it the Eucharist, that makes of me a Christian, but the love that I have for my neighbour.

(Quotes by Daniel Faivre - *Prayer of Hope of an Interfaith Man*)

Eric James, in *Collected Thoughts*, writes:

When we pray, as in this Week, for unity, peace and concord, we should be aware of the cost and effort that must inevitably accompany that prayer, if it be real and genuine.

Finally, some words from Desmond Tutu's God has a Dream:
'I HAVE A DREAM', God says, 'Please help me to realise it. It is a dream of a world whose ugliness and squalor and poverty, its war and hostility, its greed and harsh competitiveness, its alienation and disharmony are changed into their glorious counterparts, when there will be more laughter, joy, peace, where there will be justice and goodness and compassion and love and caring and sharing. I have a dream that swords will be beaten into ploughshares and spears into pruning hooks, that My children will know that they are members of one family, the human family, GOD'S FAMILY, My family. (Publisher: Rider, 2004)

Of course the ecumenical denominational scene is varied across the world and across the centuries. However, religious and cultural differences are there and when they are perceived as important parts of human, individual and community identity, they are very often a cause of unease and tension. Difference very easily leads into prejudice and may move, or be moved, from that into aggression and strife. If that is true historically for denominational differences within Christianity, it is even more so for relationships between peoples of different religions.

Time and again religion has been a central factor within violent clashes and wars between people, communities and nations. It may not be a direct cause but it has certainly been a factor in providing apparent 'legitimation' for violence and war and in 'firing people up' to make and justify personal commitment and self-sacrifice, even to deliberate suicide, for the cause.

Moreover, and it needs to be said, it is not at all only in Islam that this has been and is seen. It is something that is attached to religion and religious belief rather than to any one religion. Again, here as with denominational differences within Christianity, the scene across the world and across the centuries is varied.

THE QUESTION OF FAITH AND DENOMINATIONAL SCHOOLS

We live now in the Global Village, in an increasingly plural society with people of different cultures, histories, nationalities and races and with different religions and none.

In Britain we live also in an increasingly secular society where the differences are, we hope, gradually becoming less important and less determining socially and economically - although there is still a long way to go. But, by and large, the younger part of our population is more accepting of difference and more open to the possibilities of our lives and society being enriched by difference.

All that being so, Faith schools (schools for children of one religion) and Christian denominational schools do seem to many of us to run counter to the greater acceptance and tolerance that society and our world now need - and need urgently!

Indeed, it is more than 'tolerance' that is needed. To tolerate something or somebody or behaviour or an idea suggests putting up with something that you do not like or you think is wrong. Although that may be the case, we do need to go beyond that; to be open to, to discover, 'the dignity of difference'.

We cannot separate Christian denominational schools from Faith schools. To do so flies in the face of justice: to refuse Muslim, Jewish, Hindu, Buddhist or other Faith schools but retain Roman Catholic, Church of England, Methodist or other Christian schools would be unjust and unreal in this plural society.

Religious schools are, by their very nature, divisive. The fact that in most of Britain now this factor is much less prevalent than in Northern Ireland does not answer the problem. However good the school - and many are very good indeed, both in the school and in the community - they are symbols of division within society. Some take the plurality of religion seriously and do their best to make children aware of, and knowledgeable about, people of other denominations and other religions. But, paradoxically, it may be that the better they are equipped in those ways the greater the risk of adding to the awareness and prejudice of difference. By their very existence, religious schools may, inevitably, reinforce 'difference' in our plural society and in the minds and values of our children. Should not all education, all schools, be as free as possible of divisiveness, whether that be racial, national, cultural or religious?

There are important differences in religion between different faiths and still, if to a lesser degree, between denominations of the same religion. But, if different faiths and different denominations need to explore and explain those differences with their children, then should it be done by those faiths and those denominations in their own ways and time and at their own expense?

For all those reasons, many argue for all education, all schools, to be state education, state schools. That is surely right in the face of the history of religion and the needs of our Global Village, but there is one big condition.

Elsewhere we have spoken of, and emphasised the importance of, religion. In the UK the Christian religion has influenced, guided and nurtured so much of the development of our way of life, of our governance and of our social and individual responsibility. Therefore religion and, in the first place, the Christian religion - its history, belief and practice, and development - should be an essential part of the school syllabus. But because we are a plural society, comparative religion and the particular religious traditions and expectations of other religions present amongst us should also have an essential part in the school syllabus.

To see your grandchildren and all that excited, lively, friendly mix of children - of colour, dress, religion and culture - coming out of their state school, after having listened and learnt and celebrated together, is a joy and full of hope!

CHAPTER 2

A TYRANNY OF BELIEFS

Of course religion is not the root cause of the long-drawn-out conflict in Northern Ireland, but it is part of the background to that conflict. It is an important part and has fed and nurtured the differences that have been exploited politically, economically and socially in the history of Northern Ireland.

A similar religious, ethnic, cultural, historical mix characterised the conflicts in Bosnia, in Kosovo and in many other parts of the world. Of course there were many dissimilarities between those conflicts but, in each, religious and community 'differences' became the focus of intolerance.

Difference often creates fear. Sometimes it may simply be the fear of not understanding or of being misunderstood or just of being unable to cope with the situation, as when we meet a mentally handicapped (educationally challenged) person for the first time, or we suddenly find ourselves alone in a crowd of strangers!

Tragically, those fears can be fanned when the difference is exploited by rumour or half-truth, which have sometimes been started by, or taken up and used by, individuals or groups either genuinely believing that their way of life and community are threatened or in an opportunistic bid for power.

Those fears have often hardened into unshakeable beliefs. How often have we seen that in the history of race relations in England: 'The blacks are taking our jobs!' 'They're all on Welfare!' 'They move in and take our houses!'

It is perhaps more rare that people feel out beyond their own fears to become aware of the fears of those who have been the focus of their own fears and the butt of their own prejudices. But it does sometimes happen, as when Asian families noted the loneliness of their elderly white neighbours who were all that was left of the former community

of that estate. Their families had all moved out and away. The Asian families started calling on their white neighbours and caring for them - they evolved a sort of 'adopt a granny' scheme!
Of course religious beliefs can influence both the tragedy and the reconciliation, the prejudices and the caring - the caring acceptance of people by which the difference itself becomes changed, transformed.
But always religion and religious belief can - and, where religion is a major part of the expression or only of the infrastructure of society, will - influence both how difference is observed and how we respond to it. It may be an influence for good or evil. Across the ages and under different forms and faiths, it has been both.
On balance, then, has religious belief been for good or evil? The answer probably depends upon where you stand, at what point in history and in what place and in what community.
More disturbingly, perhaps religious belief has such a central and determining role in shaping how people see the world and each other that 'difference' is thrown into high relief and attitudes towards it are prejudiced from the outset.
To try to distance the prejudice from the belief just will not work. We cannot always see which came first, the belief or the prejudice, but we can see the ways in which belief sometimes reinforces the prejudice and sometimes institutionalises it.
Even if the Church, along with many other institutions, is working at it and getting better, Sir William Macpherson's definition of institutional racism is a relevant judgement upon us:

> *The collective failure of an organisation to provide an appropriate and professional service to people because of their colour, culture or ethnic origin. It can be seen or detected in processes, attitudes and behaviour which amount to discrimination through unwitting prejudice, ignorance, thoughtlessness and racist stereotyping which disadvantage minority ethnic people.*

In the Church of England (and not there alone) belief reinforcing prejudice has been most notable lately in relation to two groups of people. Women, and the ordination of women, is the first. In spite of eventual agreement at national level, the prejudice lingers on. Prejudices against people (or against 'principle' if that's how you see it) always linger but are not easy to maintain in face-to-face situations in which we come to know those people. So it has been with women priests and the Church. But the beliefs so vocal in Synod debates that were held to justify opposition to the ordination of women still lie uneasily behind the social and professional prejudices that women priests continue to encounter. It sometimes seems that the Church continues to harbour a belief that 'really, Jesus would have chosen some women to be apostles if God wanted women to be priests'!

Gay men are the second group. It is interesting that gay/lesbian women are not seen by the Church as a major concern. We may wonder how much that is because the beliefs nurturing the prejudices about gay/homosexual men are to do with the primacy of men over women (backed up by selected biblical passages) and the progenitive responsibilities of men (again backed up by selected biblical texts).

Homosexuality has been said to be contrary to God's law, sinful, against nature, and disordered. In Church debates 'homosexuality' has, over and over again, meant genital sex between men, in spite of the fact that homosexual relationships are primarily about relationship and not about genital acts, important as they are in the expression and nurturing of relationship. But most of the Christian Church, including the Anglicans, agree that sexual intercourse between married couples is an important expression and way of nurturing a loving, responsible relationship. Genital behaviour, then, has a purpose of unity that is acceptable and good quite apart from the reproductive purpose. The two purposes can be deliberately separated according to the mind of most of the Christian Church, including the Anglicans - but not if you are gay! And since you cannot reproduce in your homosexual relationship, sexual behaviour is disordered and wrong and you must be celibate. Your gay sexual orientation you cannot help but, under God, abstinence from sex is the only way!

True, the Church is moving away from that hard line gradually, thank God. However, this is not the place to argue the case but only to suggest how much belief nurtures and institutionalises prejudice (see the Appendix).

On the face of it, 'belief in God' (especially in the monotheism of Islam and Christianity) historically has not given a great deal of evidence of toleration, and neither has it led to a noticeable affirmation of different faith traditions. An increasing number of people, within and outwith the Church, agree that 'difference', in creed as in race and culture and sexuality, is something that calls for tolerance and affirmation. It is part of our human giftedness and therefore holds great possibilities for the enrichment of our human wholeness. But it is surely doubtful, and history gives us little encouragement to think it likely, that such toleration and affirmation depend upon theism.

The worst enemy of the search for truth in religion, and for toleration and affirmation of difference, is literalism - but literalism abounds! Because our foundation documents arise from, or have come through, a particular time, history and culture, their meaning and significance and relevance for today must be sought through reading and studying them in the two contexts of their time, history and culture and our time, history and culture.

Given the very different culture of our own time and the great reduction in worshipping members of the Church, holding on to literal understandings of traditional beliefs may well be only to court fantasy and irrelevance. However, it is not a question of ditching tradition so much as seeking non-traditional ways of understanding and maintaining tradition.

Toby went to bed on Christmas Eve expectantly, carefully hanging up his stocking. Late that night his father, standing in for Father Christmas, came into Toby's bedroom carrying a bulging stocking. Making sure that Toby was asleep, his father hung up the full stocking in place of the empty one. He then turned his attention to the sherry and mince pie thoughtfully left for Santa. He drank the sherry and bit into the mince pie - at which point an unmistakable voice from the bed

asked, "Are we enjoying it then?"
Maybe that is a relevant parable!
Belief divides. Probably that is in the nature of religion. Certainly that aspect of religion is clearly present in the Bible. But there is a danger that it is something we are prey to as human beings and as religious people who like certainties. Division does sometimes feed and strengthen our 'certainty'. So it brings temptations: strengthen the division, strengthen the 'certainty' (or vice versa). Unfortunately, religious people are sometimes more prone than others to self-righteousness, which often needs 'certainties' to prop it up!
Difference excites division - strengthens 'certainty' - justifies division - spawns self-righteousness - confirms 'difference'! It becomes a vicious circle.
It is not that religion has deliberately fomented division, although it has done that at times. But religious beliefs at times of political, social and ethnic tension have often been pressed into the service of division and violence. Sometimes religious leaders and religious institutions have led this division and conflict; sometimes it has arisen from a more popular base.
Belief may actually distort human values. Most of us would probably agree that "racism, hatred, the de-humanisation of one's fellow human beings are bad not because they can lead to Auschwitz, not even because they can lead to murder. These things are bad in and of themselves. They are unethical and unjust. Justice requires that all be treated with equal humanity" (Philip Gourevitch in *Guardian* article 4.12.99).
But are not those values part of our religious belief? Well, maybe, but sometimes that is rhetorical, and not just because it is difficult to put those values into practice. Sometimes it has been because 'belief' has been spiritualised or individualised in ways that put 'religious good' as something above or prior to the obviously 'human good' of those values.
On a television programme, hosted by Nick Ross, there were on the platform a number of well-known atheists. In the audience were many

Christians. The platform guests raised the problem of religious belief in the face of so much pain, violence and suffering. A young woman, who was a born-again Christian, was asked by Nick Ross how she would respond to that. She agreed that it was terrible, but she said that although to die in an earthquake was awful it was quick and over. What she thought was the worst suffering would be to die without God and that would be for eternity. This illustrates how belief can distort human values, and can devalue the offence of earthly pain, violence and death. Perhaps that young woman did not intend it to be so, but it sounded arrogant and self-righteous. Worryingly, there seemed to be no question in her mind about what to 'die without God' meant or what being without God 'for eternity' might mean. No doubt some viewers felt that they would rather be without God than with a God who could regard earthly human suffering, pain, violence and death with such a lack of compassion.

Some years ago a Cardinal, being interviewed on the radio, was asked what was most important goal in his life. He answered, "To save my own soul". We may know what he meant, and from one angle some may believe that it was a true and commendable response. After all, Christian life and and the following of God's way in the world will depend upon personal commitment to God and that way. However, speaking those words in the largely secular and humanist society of today will carry a very different message, probably one of the insensitivity, selfishness, self-centredness and social irrelevance of Christianity in today's world. That message, thank God, is a caricature of the Church and Christians, but, as we have seen, it has enough truth about it to stick.

Most of this chapter has illustrated what the writer has called, 'the tyranny of belief'. But that should not prevent us from claiming that belief in God is vital and necessary for any just, equitable, caring and sustainable organisation of society at all levels. However, many will find the concept of belief, especially if it puts us through unacceptable hoops like literalism, both an arid and unhelpful approach to 'faith' in God. You may think it not insignificant that the Old Testament seems to place more emphasis upon faithfulness than upon belief or the faith, i.e. the verb/action rather than the noun/concept. Commitment, in scripture as in life, does not depend upon intellectual or rational belief.

In the Church, belief is undergirded by theism, perceived as the rational belief in God. But that is part of the problem. Theism is very largely a human and social construction and one that has become the language and defence of institutional religion. Theism is therefore a cultural phenomenon and one that sociologically can be shown to be dominantly a male construction and an instrument of regulation and control of society, and thus a way of empowerment of the religious institution. That is exactly why theistic arguments relying upon logic and rationality will not motivate members of modern and largely secular societies towards belief in God.

We shall need to find new ways of showing God's relevance to culture and society and to the need for change. We shall need to find new ways of speaking about 'the truth of God' that do not depend upon arguments about 'the existence of God'. If the existence of God is to be believed, it is probably more likely to come from the practice and observation of 'Godness' than from any intellectual proofs of that existence.

The atheists and the theists both occupy the same ground. Their ritual jousting can be enjoyable and stimulating for some. But observing a ritual on a well-trodden jousting-ground with a preservation order attached to it is totally different to living a life in this complex, contradictory and challenging Global Village. So let's move away from the jousting-ground and find a possibility of thinking differently - where belief is not the measure.

The Rt Revd David Jenkins, former Bishop of Durham, used to have a diagram that suggested that 'obedience' to God's Way did sometimes unite both believers and non-believers together as Servants of the Kingdom. There could be recognition or non-recognition of Christ and of the Church, but recognisers or non-recognisers could both be serving the Kingdom, the Way, of Christ. Also, of course, there could be recognisers, Church members, who were disobedient and therefore lapsed into hypocrisy, just as there could be non-recognisers (who could not 'name' Christ) and who, in David Jenkins' phrase, 'became invincibly ignorant'.

That diagram takes us away from a central focus upon belief to a central focus upon obedience. As Grace Jantzen has expressed it, there is then a gap opening up, a possibility of thinking differently: instead of that insistence upon belief, might we not focus upon, for example, love, longing, desire and the exploration of the opening of desire that interrupts that emphasis on belief with longing for the divine horizon. That 'Godness' we spoke of is perhaps most of all there, in those thoughts and in how we explore them and follow them down the way that Christ set before us.

I came that they may have life, and have it abundantly.
(John 10:10)

He opened the book and found the place where it was written, 'The Spirit of the Lord is upon me, because he has anointed me to preach good news to the poor. He has sent me to proclaim release to the captives and recovering of sight to the blind, to set at liberty those who are oppressed, to proclaim the acceptable year of the Lord. ... Today this scripture has been fulfilled in your hearing.
(Luke 4:17-21)

AND THE FREEDOM OF FAITH

If belief can be tyrannical, just as certainly can 'faith and faithfulness' be gloriously freeing!

If we feel constrained, trapped and divided against ourselves by the expectations that we should mean literally what we say in the Creed or in the Eucharistic Prayer or read in the scriptures, then belief is far from leading us towards the glorious freedom of the sons and daughters of God. Instead, it dehumanises us. Thankfully, perhaps

most people reserve their own judgements or acknowledge to themselves their own agnosticism about various parts of scripture, creed and liturgy.
But could we not - should we not - bless and release that scepticism and agnosticism so that it might find, often through the same words, images and metaphors that wing their way to God?
"All things come from thee and of thine own have we given thee." (Words from the Offertory in the Holy Communion Service). Taken literally, that is nonsense given our knowledge thus far of the world and life. But, if taken metaphorically or symbolically, then it may have a richness of meaning way beyond that of any literal meaning.
A more humanly imaginative approach provides a space and a freedom, and indeed a grace, such that it may enrich both our humanness and our awareness of God.
Perhaps many of us who cannot think of God as Creator without numerous qualifications and limitations arising from scientific knowledge (God-given knowledge!) can nevertheless embrace with enthusiasm this phrase of Grace Jantzen's: "God is the horizon for human becoming." (*Becoming Divine* - Manchester University Press, 1998). Now that puts a different, a riskier, a challenging spin upon God as Creator!
So often the traditional, more literal approach to belief and beliefs draws us back 2000 years. There's nothing wrong with that; indeed it is necessary to ground our faithfulness upon whatever historical basis there is. But it also tends to make Christian faith, worship and awareness all too dependent upon 'memory' - the 'memory bank' of the Church. It becomes a sort of memory trick - we burnish the memory to illumine the present. But if the scriptures look beyond themselves, to Christ's coming, to the coming of the Holy Spirit, to the coming of the Kingdom (the Way) of God … then our Christian focus is here in and on this world.
By God, then, we are called into a risk business - risks in thought and action and, yes, even in faith. Those risks are not welded to 'received certainties' beyond perhaps that of St Peter and the other apostles and

disciples as they lived through the post-Crucifixion chaos, fear and threats: that somehow Christ was in this mess with them, and with them somehow even more than when Jesus was alive on earth!

We have no right deliberately to upset people by undermining their faith, but doubt is not the opposite of faith and may indeed be a gateway to faith. So doubt, when we have it, must be acknowledged and addressed. Not to do that can simply result in 'dumbing down', the closing down of what may be glorious God-given possibilities of faith and life.

Even worse than individual Christians refusing the risks of saying 'yes' to those possibilities is the attempted 'dumbing down' of the Church whenever some bishop or leading light in the Church questions traditional beliefs. There are cries from offended fellow Christians, shouts of 'heresy', murmurs of apostasy, attempts to exclude and shut down the offensive voice that has dared to doubt, to question, to de-construct the doctrines of the Virgin Birth, the physical Resurrection of Jesus, the Trinity, the Divinity of Christ, the Uniqueness of Christ, the Creator God, etc.

That response can be called a dumbing down because those questions have been commonplace in universities and colleges. Theologians have asked and studied and discussed those questions for years. There is nothing very new about them and they are serious questions that cannot be refused with integrity in this world. The price of refusal is to bury our heads in the sand and to put the Church in a ghetto.

Psychoanalyst and social philosopher Erich Fromm (1900-80) years ago wrote a book entitled *The Fear of Freedom.* Here, with the Church, as in many personal situations, dumbing down may have much to do with the fear of freedom. Is it a refusal to follow the way, God's Way, into new understanding? May it be a refusal to take risks for Christ, for faith and for our humanity?

That is not at all to say that belief and believing do not matter, but perhaps it brings to belief a biblical corrective: that faith without faithfulness is a sham. Moreover, that faithfulness means obedience to the Way of Christ, and that faithfulness is a risk and may even be at the risk of faith itself!

We have already quoted what we might call Christ's Mission Statement (John 10:10, Luke 4:17-21). Our faithfulness requires us to keep close to that, for if that is God's human project it must also be ours and it must be ours personally, socially, economically and politically, and globally. Yet, because it is only a Mission Statement it has to be understood, interpreted, worked upon and appropriated by each generation of disciples, within the context and needs of each age and situation.

Is that not what is implied by that Thanksgiving prayer after Communion? "... Send us out in the power of your Spirit to live and work to your praise and glory. Amen." That also fits perfectly with the traditional view of the Eucharist as 'our service to God' and that that 'service' necessarily calls us to 'service to people, our neighbours, God's world'.

Of course in church, in worship, that is all very symbolic and spiritual. We are saying, 'Spirit of God, Spirit of Christ, enable us, empower us for your will in the world. We have received you in Communion. Body of Christ, keep us in eternal life. Keep us in that quality of life and love, of living and loving, that we celebrated this morning. At least, keep us in the tension of that eternal life which is yours, for us, for all the world.'

That's where the real spirituality is, in the trying, the endeavour, in the way we receive and take and give the material of life, that somehow, in some part, it may resonate with God's human project. That's where the rub is: the devil is in the detail! It is so easy to be rhetorical about goodness and love and forgiveness and mercy and justice, but life is often complex and complicated. However, the darkness and the absence of God, the pain and the endurance that may accompany complexity can also carry echoes of God's human project, and God may really be present in 'his absence'.

This was written on a prison wall in Cologne by a Jewish prisoner:

I believe in the sun even when it is not shining.

I believe in love even when I cannot feel it.
I believe in God, even when He is silent.

There is another side to the problems, fears, pains and threats of complexity. The setting of Christopher Fry's *A Sleep of Prisoners*, written in the 1950s, was wartime and looking to the future, and he writes:

Thank God our time is now when wrong
Comes up to face us everywhere,
Never to leave us till we take
The largest stride of soul man ever took.
Affairs are now soul size.
The enterprise
Is exploration into God.

Although written fifty years ago, it still has a ring of truth about it, even if that exploration results in claiming that God is not real! After all, it is probably true that for centuries "monotheists in each of the God-religions had insisted that God was not merely another being" (Karen Armstrong, *A History of God*, Vintage, 1999) and that is certainly consistent with the Bible. Perhaps it is that the God we have often taken 'him/her' to be is not real. Did not the mediaevals speak of God as '*ens realismus*', or that which is most real to us?
Reality is shifting, for example, to our world and what we know about it and what we are doing to it and so to a concern about conservation, respect, and something like 'companionship' for our environment, the natural world. Along with that, there is a growing respect and responsibility towards people and countries so often exploited. Other growing realities concern our plurality of culture, sexuality, religion, colour, race and history, together with an increasing recognition of, and desire to, celebrate that.
Additional increasing realities include the opportunities for globalisation and its profits and impoverishments; the Genome Project

and all the possibilities for good and ill that it brings in its wake; the need and opportunities for expanding international unity and order, in the face of increasing division, oppression and violence. There are the realities of homes and families and of friendship and relating and parenting; of growing up in this rapidly changing world; of listening and learning and valuing … No doubt there are many more realities.

But reality is also our weakness, our sinfulness and our debilitating fear before any or all of those realities. That is the more serious if reality is where God is, or if God is not at all, but perhaps only a will-o'-the-wisp!

Now, there is a place and time for taking refuge from those realities and the Church can provide that - a time for rest, for personal stocktaking and for personal renewal ('personal' embracing both individual and society). It's a little like American poet Robert Frost's poem:

In winter in the woods alone
Against the trees I go.
I mark a maple for my own
And lay the maple low.
At four o'clock I shoulder axe
And in the afterglow
I link a line of shadowy tracks
Across the tinted snow.
I see for Nature no defeat
In one tree's overthrow
Or for myself in my retreat
For yet another blow.
(In the Clearing, Holt, Rinehart and Wincton, 1962)

If we are to respond to those realities with energy, care and hope, then the Story that the Church treasures and transmits can be an important and necessary generator for us of that energy, care and hope. Perhaps we can say, God IS the energy that sparks the possibilities for good within those realities. But God IS also the Story that is entrusted to the

Church.
Can that help us get away from the aridity of 'belief' that all too often saddles people with what may be not so much Godly burdens as man-made shibboleths?
Just as the Service to God in the Eucharist should issue in service to people and the world, so prayerful attention to God in the Story should issue in prayerful attention to God's Way in the mêlée of changing realities. 'The Word was made flesh': The Word was made reality, and brings immense possibilities for good.
We are saying that many of what have been the 'required', traditional understandings of God are trammels that may confine and impede faith, and that belief is then a tyranny. That is how many people see it and therefore reject the Church, and often any idea of faith with it. But in spite of its shortcomings, the Church is the guardian and transmitter of the Christian Story. There often still remains for many, some belief in God; a conviction that there is something important that religion is about. But, in a way, it might be said that the Church has disenfranchised them by appearing to confine the sense and meaning of God, religion and spirituality to its own traditional and literal messages,  images and definitions. The great rise in New Age and other alternative spiritualities (many around alternative or complementary medicines or therapies) may be a measure of that disenfranchisement and also of spiritual hunger.
Many people are very happy with, and enabled and strengthened by, traditional beliefs and literal understandings of them in the Church. There is a Quaker phrase about 'speaking to their condition' and that would mean, in that case, to respect and encourage those people 'where they are'. George Fox (1624-91), founder of the Religious Society of Friends (Quakers), told Quaker reformer William Penn to "wear thy sword as long as thou canst". In other words, do not change until you are clear that that is what your conscience requires of you.
But are there not also other 'conditions' to which we ought to be speaking, other people who can no longer wear those swords, which for them - under the Spirit of God - are no longer swords of truth!

CHAPTER 3

A PROPOSAL: A WAY AHEAD

We need to be more radical and to say clearly that all religion is a human and social construction. But then we need to go on to say that nevertheless all religion seems to be based upon, or to arise from, some genuine human sense that 'there is more'. A sense that 'there is something else', 'something more than', 'something other than' this life, this experience, this knowledge, these limitations...!

From that point we suggest that the religious sense is a questing sense and that religion, whatever else, is always a question mark. However, religion as a human construction has soon and usually concerned itself with making answers. To do that, religions have established special people and, in time, special institutions, whose speciality is discovering and determining the answers and providing ways of disseminating those answers. But the answers are ever more sophisticated and developed human constructions. Nonetheless it may be true that much of the work and worship of religious institutions does meet with, and clarify and enhance, that basic human religious sense of 'the more', 'the beyond' and 'the other'.

However, in all religions it is probably the core Stories (i.e., particularly the Gospels, in Christianity) that meet most clearly and resonate most clearly with that basic human religious sense. In other words, STORY NOT THEOLOGY is the basic motivation of religious faith and practice.

Unfortunately, the religious institutions have tried, all too frequently, to control and channel the Stories so that they fit the current phase of our human religious construction - and the questing spirit is discouraged. But what if it is just that questing, questioning spirit that is most closely allied to those Stories and to that basic religious sense? Churches and religious institutions need to ask themselves if it is not perhaps 'their religion' that drives people away; meaning by 'their religion' the human and institutional construction put upon whatever basic religious sense and story there is.

In so far as God is the subject of religion, then it follows from the above that God is a human construction. But, in so far as God is more than that, corresponding to 'the more', 'the beyond', 'the other' of human desire, then God is more than simply a human construction.

Maybe the present popularity of New Age philosophies and spiritualities, astrology and the many individualised and commercialised attempts to find and cultivate ideas of the 'inner me' and the 'mystic reality' are symptoms of a human unease with the collapse of the supernatural. Might that be because the supernatural has been collapsed into the religious institution?

Let us suggest that the supernatural, or the transcendent, is locationally a misnomer and that it is in fact an integral dimension of our humanness. If so, we shall need to find or rediscover how to celebrate it there; how to use and celebrate that dimension of our humanness.

However, being an integral dimension of our humanness does not necessarily mean that it is wholly contained by our humanness - any more than love can be said to be wholly contained by our humanness. T. S. Eliot's "... the drawing of this Love and the voice of this Calling ..." is a reality of human experience. (Four Quartets, Little Gidding).

Is it not that we need more questing and questioning and fewer answers? Perhaps religion needs to learn that from the astrophysicists, the environmental scientists - humbled by time and space!

A major task of theology must be to shape the framework within which the Story may be understood and its relevance to the religious sense be explicated and that 'sense' be stimulated. So may that basic religious sense be encouraged and enabled to engage with the realities and particularities of life and living in the new and future time. Is that not also what worship and liturgy are about, or are called to be about?

We have emphasised the prior importance of the religious sense, the questing nature of that sense and the Stories that resonate with that religious sense. If we are right in that emphasis, then our imagination is engaged in the exercise, development and application of that

religious sense.
But religious traditions, Church governance and discipline, and 'official' theology have sought to speak 'scientifically' - i.e., as though describing observed facts. So belief became prescribed beliefs. Belief requiring and welcoming imagination was never central to the Church except within its own liturgical and ceremonial expression.
Imagination is a way, sometimes the only way, of gaining insight to belief; of giving flight to faith, to wing its way into the vast realities and uncertainties of life and death in all the complex relationships of our universe.
It is not sufficient to leave that task to artists and imaginative scientists. Open to all that, stimulated and inspired by those artists and scientists, there is a MINISTRY OF IMAGINATION that the Church needs to cultivate.

Hopefully, what follows may contribute to that ministry of imagination.

CHAPTER 4

AWARENESS: THE HUMAN DRAMA

No, I do not believe that there ever was a Golden Age in some Garden of Eden. Neither do I believe in the literal and historical truth of any other part of the Creation, Innocence and Fall stories in the book of Genesis. However, as metaphors of life and meaning I find them very rewarding, exciting and true. Therefore what follows is not biblical scholarship but imagination: the work of, I hope, a critical imagination upon the stories and upon my own experience.

We start with a glorious account of the Creation, of the coming of form and shape, of light and dark and the emergence of our universe. Then God creates life of all sorts and variety, including the life of humankind. Humans God created in his own image and male and female he created them. God gave them responsibility - is that perhaps what being made in God's own image meant?

Crowning all those gifts of Creation, finally, to humans God gave responsibility - a trust and a charge: to be good stewards, to respect and care for all that created universe. That is the responsibility that George Macleod, founder of the Iona Community, called 'the scientists' charter'.

Although the first Creation story, in Genesis chapter 1, speaks of subduing the earth and having dominion over every living thing, that does not imply the exploitation and carelessness of modern mankind (the choice of gender here is deliberate) towards the created world. Whatever the detail, the pattern and movement of the Creation stories are of givenness and goodness: "And God saw everything that he/she had made, and behold, it was very good."

In the detail of the second account (Genesis chapter 2), there is a lovely picture of God forming every beast and bird and bringing them one by one to the human "to see what he would call them". Whatever he chose, those would be their names. There may be magical power connotations here, through naming and claiming, but there may be other lessons for us. Not magical but a more intimate and caring scene: we are not so easily exploitative and careless of those we meet face to face and name.

All this GIVENNESS is glorious! This glory, this what we might call 'ordinary glory', is beautifully painted for us in the image of "the Lord God walking in the garden in the cool of the day." Human beings, men and women, companying with God as the sun goes down and the heat of the day expires and people, with God, relax!

But that was not to last. The humans had eaten of the tree in the middle of the garden, the tree of the knowledge of good and evil, for "God knows that when you eat of it your eyes will be opened, and you will be like God, knowing good and evil." So they were driven out of the Garden of Eden.

What a parable of life! It is like a Greek tragedy, where the tragedy is inevitable - an inevitable part and result of growing up. The innocence of children must go if, as adults, we are ever to become as little children.

To put it another way: if the Garden of Eden is the 'good life', it is nevertheless unknowable as the 'good life' until you have left it, in the agony of loss. The tree in the middle of the garden, of the knowledge of good and evil, and the loss of innocence, can be seen as the inevitable development of self-consciousness and self-awareness and, with it, the ability to choose. "The eyes of both were opened, and they knew that they were naked …."

Questioning and scepticism follow, and humankind, delivered by the Fall - yes, ironically, 'delivered' by the Fall - starts its pilgrimage towards the reality, the 'good life', the God of which and of whom it has some dim and nagging awareness. Like some lodestone, human beings seem drawn to some greater purpose, some greater life.

Here we start our adventure into life and love. An experience common to many families provides a similar metaphor, a reminder of the Creation stories: a child - the birth; that miraculous gift-child! Later, she goes to her first school, making that incredibly huge step, venturing eyes agog towards all that new experience, on tiptoe, expectant, a little fearful, absorbing all that comes. Then home, darting up the path, already pouring out, helter-skelter, all the doings of the day. How come? Her confidence for that adventure bubbles out from the love in which she is held and nurtured.

However, that changes, and must change, if the child is to become the adult. The adventure is, in a sense, by love out of love and into life - and love; only now it's a struggle as self-consciousness and awareness move into self-concern and self-interest. It is no long trip from there to using people and things for our own gratification or advertisement. We may cease to hear the cries of our self; our self-consciousness may no longer delight in the sights and sounds and life around us that tease, tug, test and draw us out to new adventures. Now, those things too easily may become not waymarks of our adventure into life and love but trophies to hang upon our armour.

The exploitations and dominations of our world, its people and its creatures, are but the extension of that fearful adventure. The first violence, of Cain and Abel; the chaos and disorder that preceded the Flood; the great machismo of the Tower of Babel - these are all metaphors for that same fearful adventure that is our human drama.

It is true that not all that denies and destroys the gift of universe and life, but it often denies and destroys the gift-relationship. And there can be no relationship except if we 'receive' the gift. That is where the story of the Prodigal Son (Luke ch. 15) is such a purposeful and powerful metaphor.

When the son, who had left home and wasted his inheritance (all the gifts with which he was laden) in riotous living, in a far country, 'came to himself', he turned home. No sooner had he turned towards home, even though he was in a far country, and before he had murmured any words of regret or apology, the father was there, welcoming him with open arms. That was all that was needed: to come to himself, or herself, and turn homewards.

Home means so many things. It means myself, loved - warts and all, vulnerable but valued. It means God who accepts and loves unconditionally: God, the Life, the giver of all that I have been running away from, or denying, or hitting. It means the company of those whose acceptance and love lead me into a gift-relationship, echoing that first Creation. It means this world, this universe, this ecosystem - not to destroy or exploit, but to notice and attend to, to delight in, protect, nurture and celebrate.

That seems to be not the end of our adventuring but the opening of new doors, the sight of long vistas of new possibilities. Here we seem to touch upon the mystery of the Resurrection, the possibilities of life qualitatively, as different from life as cheese from chalk or wine from water. There perhaps, between the wind, we may hear the sound of the Lord God walking in the garden in the cool of the day.

These metaphors for the human drama are not, as I understand them, about an historical progression or the ordered progress of individual life, but are echoes of the movements of the soul - not that clinical, hygienic, 'religious' spirit-soul, but the soul that is the very heart of our longing, feeling, curious being.

They indicate the ebbing and flowing of human awareness, the darkness and light through which, and by which, we must find our way - for somehow we know there is a way.

CHAPTER 5

HUMBLED BY TIME

'DINOSAURS SHRUNK THE MILLENNIUM!'

Why have dinosaurs held such a fascination for our children? True, there has been a huge commercial package built upon the back of dinosaurs, and children are a large market via indulgent parents. So perhaps, like the diabolo, spinning-tops, jacks and the yo-yo, they are a passing fancy.

Mega-creatures are in all the world's myths and stories, including elephants before children discovered dinosaurs, and megastars of screen, cartoon, football pitch and pop scene always seem to attract and fascinate. Thus 'mega' becomes an important selling point that has been exploited very successfully. But that fancy with T Rex, Triceratops, Stegosaurus *et al.* has a more serious side.

Dinosaur Detectives one afternoon on BBC One probably came as a surprise to mere adults and revealed the ignorance of grandparents! It was not a cartoon, but rather was presented imaginatively as an adventure of a group of children, who were the detectives. They visited diverse sites and various experts across the world. Theirs was a serious, intelligent enquiry into the existence and demise of dinosaurs. It did not provide any easy answers; the debate continues and there remain a number of possible causes of the extinction of the dinosaurs. Many children are now well aware of the life, characteristics and differences between the various dinosaurs, their lifestyles and the possible explanations as to what happened to them.

Is it not intriguing that children are so fascinated by creatures that inhabited this world a hundred million years ago? Is it not equally intriguing that they can carry and cope with the serious doubts and possibilities of the dinosaur debate? Intriguing particularly because

how difficult it is to find adults who are as able to carry and cope with the doubts and possibilities that surround the people and events of the beginning of Christianity only two thousand years ago!
In one sense of time, dinosaurs do indeed shrink the millennium. They inhabited the Earth for around a hundred million years, whereas humankind has been on Earth less than one million years - and could well extinguish itself in less than half the length of time the dinosaurs bestrode the Earth. However, even the dinosaur's lifespan on Earth was small within the total scale of life on Earth, which is something like four thousand million years - give or take a million years or so.
Do films like *Jurassic Park* try to give us a hold on 'dinosaur time' by shrinking the time in our favour? If we can by our modern bio-technology actually procure the birth of the long extinct dinosaur, and another and another, and herd them all in a great theme park, we shall bring them into our time where we can watch, study, control .... Human beings shall then appear much more important in the scale of time - what a conceit! Is it an echo of the Church's opposition to Copernicus and Galileo?
Perhaps our children can teach us humility, or maybe it is innocence before the glory of Creation.

> *You never enjoy the world aright, till the sea itself floweth in your veins, till you are clothed with the heavens, and crowned with the stars: and perceive yourself to be the sole heir of the whole world, and more than so, because men are in it [and women], who are every one sole heirs as well as you. Till you can sing and rejoice and delight in God, as misers do in gold, and kings in sceptres, you never enjoy the world.*
> *(Thomas Traherne, d. 1674, Centuries: 1st Century [29])*

OUR FEET IN A LARGE ROOM!

One of the problems of the way in which the Bible has often been regarded is that it seems to suggest that all of God and all of Christ are contained within those pages and within that time. However, greater awareness of the scientific, tentative and agnostic approach to the beginnings and evolution of the universe, the Earth and life on Earth, including human life, would invite us to take a more humble view.

We should listen to David Hope, Archbishop of York, alongside of Thomas Traherne:

> Two thousand years on, everything has changed in the sense of technological progress. But in a more fundamental sense, nothing has changed. As God was, so he still is and ever will be.
> Our perception of his changelessness, however, has changed. We know now that this is also the God within the power of whose being there pulses the heartbeat of a thousand million galaxies, and within the minutiae of whose caring lies every atomic particle of the air we breathe.
> (*Guardian*, 'Face to Faith', 18.12.99)

It is true, of course, that the visionary imagery of the Bible in the Creation stories (in the first book of the Bible), and in the Prologue to St John's Gospel, and in chapters 21 and 22 of the Revelation to John (the last book of the Bible), show us a wide and inclusive picture of the timespan of the universe, and all contingent upon God. In that sense the 'all of God' is contained within the Bible, but only if we have the imagination to let God be God, neither confined by nor restricted to the Bible, nor indeed to the Christian religion or to any religion.
Yet some Christian understandings of the Bible suggest that 'all of Christ - God incarnate' is contained within those pages alone. The problem then is that we make our God too small and too exclusive, and, whereas that may be good for our egos if we call ourselves Christian, it does nothing for human unity and growth in human understanding.
There are also more problems, in that we can appear to set Christ

(contained within the pages of the Bible) against God, who clearly spills over and will not be constrained by the Bible. It is small wonder that the Church has found the Holy Spirit a difficult and uncomfortable reality!

However, this constricting biblicism about Christ is a product of the Church rather than the Bible itself because, as with God so with Christ, the Bible shows a Christ who is much greater, more inclusive, more universal than some Church traditions allow. The following are a few indicators of that from one Gospel (it has to be admitted that it is easier to find them in John than elsewhere):

In the beginning was the Word, and the Word was with God and the Word was God ... and the Word was made flesh ...
(John 1:1,14)

... before Abraham was, I am ...
(John 8:58)

... and I, when I am lifted up from the earth, will draw all men to myself.
(John 12:32)

... when the Comforter is come, whom I will send unto you from the Father, even the Spirit of truth, which proceedeth from the Father, he shall bear witness of me.
(John 15:26)

This has not been a plea to take the Bible less seriously but, in fact, to take it more seriously - although perhaps less earnestly! Do we not need to see the Bible in the context of something much wider and much more developmental? The Bible is a record and a recollection, in a particular time, of God's self-disclosure through the mists of history, circumstance and culture. It is also the record of man's and woman's reaching out towards, longing for, and sometimes misunder-

standing or ignoring of that disclosure. And that disclosure reaches out well beyond the particular time warp of the historic moment of the Bible.
Come on children and your dinosaurs, introduce us, so that we also might enjoy that glorious vastness and be teased by possibility!
Then let us, in God's name, take our humanity in all its plurality with the seriousness of God's givenness. In that awareness let us explore and enjoy the variety and the treasury of God-given humanity.
The sense of possibility, the possibilities before us of human growth and development - is that not another way of speaking about the Providence of God?
Let me finish with some appropriate words of Bobby Kennedy (d. 1968), US politician and statesman, quoted at his funeral by his brother Edward:

Some men see things that are and say, "Why?"
I dream things that never were and say, "Why not?"

THE ICE MAN COMETH!

A relative of ours lay down upon a freezing stone high up in the Austrian Tyrol, and died. Was it a heart attack or hypothermia that overcame him? Was he, as some suggested, the Italian music professor who had disappeared in 1941 on the same route as those climbers in 1991 had discovered that corpse rising out of the glacier?
We now know he was not the music professor but an unknown relative of his and ours who died some 3,000 years before Jesus. Innsbruck University has dated the 'Ice Man' from the Neolithic period, about 5,200 years ago.
Now ask yourself some questions:

* If you think of him as dying that lonely death 50 years ago, how do you picture it in your mind?

* Then you discover that it was in fact 5,200 years ago that he died. So now how do you picture it in your mind?

* Perhaps the images were different, but did they feel very different?

Or suppose you are fortunate enough to stand before the 30,000-year-old cave paintings in Chauvet: don't the years, the aeons, shrink as some sense of relationship, of kinship, of identity well up in your consciousness?
Certainly there is an awareness of immensity, like gazing at the heavens in a starlit night sky. But there is a difference. The immensity of the universe, which fills us with awe as we quietly scan the heavens, may also make us feel how small, how insignificant we are in the vast 'scheme of things'. How tiny we are and what little space, place and time we occupy as we see that distant star and realise that what we see is thousands of light years away from the 'present' reality of that star. The present tense is a long, long way into our future!
But the awe that we feel before those cave paintings and before the 5,200-year-old Ice Man may be quite different to the awe that the stars kindled in us. There is a vastness, an immensity of time, and yet there is an immediacy, the shock of a relationship that puts our humanity in a different and responsible relationship.
'I was there' in a sense, and 'he is here', sharing the same hopes, fears and desires. The long thread of life looping across the years; telegraph wires singing down 5,000 and 30,000 years!
Where then was the Christ?

A STRANGE AND TRAGIC TAPESTRY

Eintragen in das Verzeichnis der
Gefangenembucherei unter Nr. 1291

That is stamped on the flyleaf of a book entitled *Albrecht Dürer*, which

I 'liberated' (as the jargon went) from the S.S. quarters of Westerbork Camp on the Dutch/German border. It is a fascinating, well-illustrated book about the life and work of German painter and engraver, Albrecht Dürer (1471-1528).
The flyleaf stamp is not significant, although as I look at that number I remember another number - a number that was burnt onto the wrist of a boy I knew at school. Peter had been branded and shackled in a Concentration Camp. He had seen his twin sister abused and killed before his eyes. He was himself, later, thrown into a burial ditch from which he crawled out, eventually managing to get to England and a Quaker School. Peter was Jewish, the son of the leader of a famous orchestra. After I had left school I heard that Peter had committed suicide. I do not believe that he was led to that only by his horrifying experiences in the Camp. At school he was a difficult boy to like and to get on with, which is not surprising. But in the late 1930s/early 1940s, to English schoolboys, the experiences and the plight of Jewish refugees must have been 'unreal'. There was little empathy with and little sensitivity towards Peter and he was often bullied.
That book and that insignificant library number make the connection. How that stealing stole into the tragic lives of many Jewish families - Peter and his family and all those who were sent from Westerbork Camp to Auschwitz and the gas chambers. Jewish diarist Anne Frank and Hetty Hillesum (also a diarist: Etti: A Diary 1941-1943, Ape 1983) were amongst those Jews from Amsterdam for whom Westerbork was a staging-camp.
It was 1945 and I was a young man, a conscientious objector and member of The Friends' Ambulance Unit. Section 6 F.A.U. had just moved to take responsibility for an adjacent Camp, Walchem, with the inevitable 'Arbeit Macht Frei' (Work Makes Freedom) splashed across its entrance.
The Camp at Walchem was a Displaced Persons' Camp that housed a mixture of Russian, Polish, Italian and Czech people. Some were prisoners of war, but most were forced labourers. The Polish Division (British Army) initially guarded the Camp, but moved off as we

organised the Camp, set up a Camp Committee, chose a Camp Commandant and a Medical Officer and established working parties, which set about dismantling the barbed-wire fences and the machine-gun and lookout posts and turning sentry boxes into latrines.
It was an optimistic and wonderful time, an international Camp, working together and in a small way building a more hopeful future. That was what it seemed like. But down the road was Westerbork Camp, deserted then except for two men we discovered, pyjama-striped and ill. We took them to hospital.
Only years later did I realise what a strange and tragic tapestry of lives and loves and fears was woven into those few miles of the Dutch/German border. Leafing through that book is a constant reminder of them: how time and chance bring us into each other's orbit; how choices made lead us unbeknown and often unrecognised into places, circumstances and situations of happiness and pain, unbearable sadness, violence and death, made uniquely significant by the lives, personalities and possessions of particular people thrown together or torn apart by happenstance.
Time is not at all a regular sequence of hours, months, years, a straight line or row of events one after another. Neither is it only an inexorable passage of moments. In spite of the clock, moments dance, stagger, stay, return and run on.

LURE OF ORCHIDS

Orchids are a late arrival on the botanic scene. The earliest evidence of the orchid is a fossil in Germany dated to the Miocene epoch, 15 million years ago. But most plants can be traced back 60 to 100 million years. Because they are late on the scene, they are young in the evolutionary journey and are still evolving.
In the genus *Ophrys* especially, this continuing evolution is quite easy to see. There is an increased specialisation in the relationship between the flower and the pollinator. The more exactly the flower corresponds

to the needs and behaviour of the pollinator, the more certain will be the reproduction of the species. Thus there are orchid flowers that resemble bees - bees of different sorts, flies, spiders, butterflies and other insects, and have adapted themselves to attract particular pollinators. Not only are they adapted to attract by shape, colour and scent, but also their form is adapted to make sure that the animal pollinator, whatever it is, does the job required. So the sexual organs of the flower are arranged so that the pollen sacs are certain to attach to the animal and are only likely to be brushed off as the bee or fly or whatever goes to another flower of the same species. There some of the pollen will attach to the stigma of the other flower. And to do that successfully the flower shape has had to adapt to the shape and manner of the particular insect.

The adaptation goes further. Some flowers look as though they contain luscious nectar when in fact they do not, but it serves the purpose of attracting the pollinator. Others deceive in different ways: some have managed to produce a scent resembling female pheromones; they have become sexual mimics. Some even look so like the insect, and perhaps also aided by the pheromone scent, that they dupe the insect into full sexual behaviour. As it attempts to copulate, so the flower has it in the right place and with sufficient time to ensure the transfer of the pollen sacs to the right part of the insect's body.

But what happens when fertilisation becomes harder because fewer of those required insect pollinators are around, perhaps because of use of insecticides or for whatever other reason?

The orchids try to adapt to the changing circumstances and so, in some cases, flowers on a stem may become fewer because that increases the chance of becoming fertilised. Or they may change in shape, colour or scent. Perhaps hybridisation is an adaptation that will increase the opportunities for fertilisation. These continual evolutionary adaptations are, we may suppose, one reason why orchids are so often being reclassified - mostly according to the insects that enable the reproduction of the plant.

Time past and time future are indeed both present in time now!

Is that one reason why some of us are fascinated, and humbled, by the lure and the wonder of orchids - not the cultivated ones but the ones you can find by yourself in their natural habitat and which often take a lot of tracking down.

Is it not the same for human beings? Are we not still evolving? After all, we have only been around for less than a fifteenth of the time that orchids have been on the Earth. Are we not still adapting to new circumstances and changing in order to do so? What a speed of changing life and circumstance we have experienced this century, or even over the last fifty years. All right, we may not adapt ourselves by changing our shape or developing new limbs. Perhaps it is more likely, since unlike the orchid we have consciousness and minds and the ability to envisage and affect the future, that it is by tools and technologies that we adapt to new circumstances. The tools and technologies become, as they always have, an extension of our own humanity. In these days of information technology, of mobile phones, laptop computers, the Internet and the email, is it really too difficult to think perhaps that there is in this a significant evolutionary step that human beings are making?

Perhaps the Genome Project, the mapping of the human genes, and the technology that will enable that information to be used to prevent certain inherited diseases and disabilities might be another evolutionary step for humanity.

It may well be, we are told, that medical scientific advances will enable the body to heal itself, to produce healthy new cells to replace damaged or worn-out ones. Already, apparently, skin cells from an old man have been 'rejuvenated' by incorporating the healing ability that enables a lizard to grow its own new tail. Cell rejuvenation as we age! Is that to be an indicator of a new evolutionary step? 'Indefinite life extension': that was a phrase used in a BBC programme recently.

What a prospect, full of wonderful yet horrifying possibilities! To choose the possibilities, to judge rightly, to pursue wisely and caringly and within the context of the Global Village and its needs, we must allow ourselves to be humbled by time, or human arrogance will be

unbearable by the Earth.
Human beings may blow up their world. They may become extinct by their own hands. However, other species have become extinct in the history of our world, and yet the world continues. The Earth has suffered many cataclysmic misfortunes in the course of its generation. Yet to call them 'misfortunes' is, as it were, to perceive them through our eyes, and since the Earth has only accommodated humans for a very, very, tiny, passing moment of its existence, to call those massive changes in the span of the Earth's life 'misfortunes' would be human arrogance in the extreme.
Human beings, human societies, may accelerate the Greenhouse Effect, may in many another way destroy the world as we know it, including human life on Earth, and may cause massive changes to the Earth. But, in all probability, the Earth will continue its place in the universe; the Earth will, as before, adjust to the new conditions. Life will regenerate or continue and grow as it did after the dinosaurs were exterminated.
For us, for humanity, for human society to be humbled by time must surely mean to be humbled by God's Time. That is not aethereal nonsense. It means much more than the clock; it means something about relationship and contingency and opportunity. Does it not mean something about the recognition of interdependence and of what the mystics have always described as the unity in which we and all life and all nature are held together?

WHAT IF BOSCH ISN'T BOSH?

In the fifteenth century, Hieronymous Bosch painted a Millennium Tryptych of which the right-hand panel is Hell. John Berger suggests that "this hell has become a strange prophecy of the mental climate imposed on the world at the end of our twentieth century, by globalisation and the new economic order" (*Guardian* article, 20.11.99). He may be right. If so, that would be an odd trick that time

had played upon us.
How can that wild, flat, horrific painting of fire, destruction, indignity, frenetic activity prolonging torture and endless suffering, be a true prophecy for our world in the new millennium?
However, it is not in the detail of his tortures and torture machines that Bosch may be a true prophet, but rather in the design of his painting. It is perhaps in the despair and the reduction of humanity: reduced to naked, bent, separated and unrelated figures intent upon, unable to avoid, frenetic activity going nowhere. There is, as Berger points out, no horizon there; no pauses, no continuity between actions. It seems full of pointless surprises and interruptions and it screams silently at us. Yet there is no silence, no dignity - 'no time to stand and stare'.
Is that the scene that globalisation conjures up?
Hell may be a myth, but it is a very powerful myth and a myth that has often been useful to the Church as a control agent. It was, and for some people still is, a bit like an offender wearing an electronic tag: it's a constant threat, a constant reminder. But if we demythologise and then remythologise hell, perhaps we can say that hell is where God is not.
Now whatever else God is, God is relationship. Indeed, in the Christian faith tradition, 'relationship' is seen to be at the very core, of the very essence, of God - Father, Son and Holy Spirit. On the contrary, Bosch's Hell is a place of total unrelationship, where people are reduced to individual ciphers, only defined by the hell they inhabit.

Globalisation sounds wonderful: the growing awareness of the Global Village we live in; the commitment to production for the good, the benefit of all; the commitment to sharing and to building a more equal and a more caring world; stewarding the natural resources of land, sea and air for the benefit of future generations and the ecological well-being of the planet. Unfortunately, that is not what globalisation is about, and while it is finance led, profit led, USA- and European-interest led, then it is never likely to be what globalisation is about.
Unfortunately, the reality of globalisation today is more about manipulating and using skills, resources and labour, especially where they may be had more cheaply, to increase the generation and

distribution of commodities. It's about the globalisation of trade - but, so far, the terms of trade between countries are always determined by the powerful, the wealthy, the Western nations, and determined in their favour.
Globalisation is about global financial markets. If that sounds like 'equal opportunities' for all nations, have another think. These markets are most likely operated by faceless people and their computers in air-conditioned offices in some major financial centres of the world (presumably mainly in the USA, Europe and Japan) - global financial markets that are accountable to nothing that could be called representative of real, global, human interests.
It is very likely that John Berger is more or less correct in saying: "Globalisation is merely the totalitarian extension of the logic of the finance markets to all aspects of life." So what does that do to the world's poor? What does that do to the world's relatively, or in some cases obscenely, wealthy?

Time hath, my Lord, a wallet at his back.
(William Shakespeare, *Troilus and Cressida*, 1602)

CHILD TIME

So different - the time of children. Time is not measured in pounds and pence; it is not measured in the ticking clock or the calendar. But it may be immensely greater, longer and more unbearable than for you and I - those adults.

* For young children, time is the presence, the assurance and security of mummy and daddy - then time is short.
* For young children time is the absence of mummy or daddy; then is the void, the longing, the fear unendurably endless.

Children's timescales and our adult timescales are quite different. We play peek-a-boo with little children, we disappear for a moment and then quickly reappear - 'peek-a-boo'. Gradually, the child learns that her mummy and daddy always come back, are always there for her, even if they are hidden from her vision for a while. She comes to know and to trust that she is always loved. Unless something destroys that trust, she can grow and thrive because she is borne up by that assurance. Because she sees it, learns it from her parents and family, she knows she has 'worth' - she is an esteemed and valued little person in her own right. So she can grow with the sense of her own worth, her self-esteem as an individual, individuating and developing her own gifts, skills and abilities.

But sometimes that trust is destroyed and her world falls apart, and now no game of peek-a-boo can bring her assurance and security. Or maybe it does for a while because again her mummy is there for her: she was mistaken, "Mummy's back!" But if that loss becomes a pattern, then the reappearances probably become less and less convincing. If it also includes a pattern of neglect, then she (let's call her Sam) is going to feel more alone, more disturbed and more unloved.

How long those weeks and months must be - long for Sam's mother, who loves her, but is in trouble and uncertain and can't get it together, but much, much longer for Sam.

So Sam may be taken into Care (on a statutory or voluntary basis). Whilst in Care there may be great efforts by social workers to work with Sam's parents in order to help them work through their problems so that Sam may return to them. But it make take a long time to turn around some of the problems, and a long time to rebuild the mother's self-esteem and confidence.

Sam may be returned to her family too early and then have to be removed again into Care, or perhaps this time placed with foster carers. Indeed, as various workers strive to help, assist and mend the breaches in family life that caused Sam to be removed, Sam may have a number more moves, back home again, or to other foster carers ....

Remember how Sam's time experience was so dependent upon the presence or the absence of mummy and daddy being there for her? How then must Sam feel now? What have these moves, these different carers, these weeks and months and possibly years, the longings and hopes and fears Sam has, done to her self-worth, her self-esteem now? Probably you and I have learnt to wait; experience may have taught us patience, but even that depends a lot upon the quality of our own relationships. But children can't wait - not for love or for permanent parenting, not without doing them immense damage. In childcare work, in fostering and adoption work, everyone knows that. So, in British law, the child's welfare and interest is paramount.

Must that not also imply that the child's time too is paramount, above the time, interests, habits and disciplines of adults and adult institutions? If we are thinking of a happy, well-adjusted child in a loving and supportive family, then that emphasis is less vital for that child's time and the adults' time will be closer, by the relationships they enjoy. Also, because through the confidence engendered in that child by those loving relationships, he or she will be able to be more tolerant of adults' time.

But for Sam, her welfare and interests must be paramount. She wants - needs - permanency of parenting and 'there-for-ever' parents - only then can she grow into her birthright of life, that spring of life that can nurture and cultivate her own unique personality and its possibilities for happiness and fulfilment.

So the big question remains: how can we so organise our childcare, our adoption and fostering agencies, the courts and all the other agencies and institutions that affect choices for Sam in such a way that her welfare and interests (which must include Sam's 'time') really are the paramount consideration and the paramount factor in determining the plan and the timing of the plan for Sam.

Time is, for all of us, so much more than duration. Perhaps that is what is implied by the term 'quality time', which parents try to ensure that they have with their children. The trouble is that in a sense all time is quality time. What the quality is, whether good or bad, helpful or unhelpful, may be the more important question. Further, can we -

should we - programme our children to arrive bushy-tailed and bright-eyed for our quality time hour? Is that how their 'time' needs it?

CHAPTER 6

BECOMING WARM FLESH

The Word was made flesh and dwelt among us ...
(John 1:14)

Within me even the most metaphysical problem takes on a warm physical body which smells of sea, soil and human sweat. The Word, in order to touch me, must become warm flesh. Only then do I understand - when I can smell, see and touch.
(Nikos Kazantzakis, *Report to Greco*)

Christianity has operated best not through Popes, Moderators, and assorted Holy Roman Geezers, but through ordinary punters who never thought of themselves as doing anything very special. I thank God for them.
(Ron Ferguson, article in *Glasgow Herald*, 1.1.00)

The Greek word used in John's Gospel for 'flesh' is apparently the same word that was used for meat - no avoidance, no distancing, no pretending there, but a thoroughly down-to-earth statement.
'God in Man' (in humanity) 'made manifest' - in human beings, in women, men and children, to be made manifest? No wonder, we also sing at Christmas: "The hopes and fears of all the years are met in Thee tonight" (*O Little Town of Bethlehem*).
Not only are minds and intellects to be kindled, but also bodies, emotions and imaginations, set alight by that revelation of God's Love, of God's Givenness.

O God, fan to flame in me and in your Church the fire of your life ...
(Church of South India)

The fire of your life, of your relationship, of your giving, your affirming, your joy!

Is that the same sense, the same feeling, that is manifesting its need and hunger when in worship people express their emotions freely in song and dance and in more ecstatic ways? A black Gospel choir, a Caribbean congregation, vibrate with an infectious enthusiasm. Unfortunately, perhaps, many of us stiff-upper-lipped, reserved Anglo-Saxons do not take kindly to too much enthusiasm in our worship! But to sit in the rafters of Altenberger Catholic/Protestant Dom, listening to Beethoven's *Missa Solemnis* with a packed congregation of young people who had slept the night in the surrounding woods, was a not too dissimilar experience.

However, it is also present - that need for the Word to become warm flesh in order to touch me - when we commit our church and ourselves to Christian Aid work, CAFOD, Oxfam, etc., or to addressing the needs of homeless people on our streets, or working on issues of poverty with Church Action on Poverty, or tackling Third World debt issues and urging their cancellation by our government. It is present whenever we feel the need, and do something about it, to work out some true correspondence between our worship, our faith and the way we live in the world, in our neighbourhood and in our homes.

It was with the Friends' Ambulance Unit and Relief Service in Oberhausen in the Ruhr that I felt most strongly that our work did truly correspond with our faith and did really spring from and was energised by our worship - a simple, daily, Quaker prayer time. Then back out to get involved in all the civilian relief work of food distribution, of medical services for people living in the bunkers, of children's nurseries, youth work, holiday camps, IVSP (International Voluntary Service for Peace) Work Camps; of doing all this alongside German town and church officials.

But, of course, I was younger; it was 1946/7 just after the war, and it was all much simpler and more direct than most of the situations in which we find ourselves now. Now, the competing needs, complications and complexities of living, in peacetime, in Britain, in the Third Millennium are greater. But also the need now is even greater.

The danger now in this Global Village of a world is that we become overwhelmed by the world's pain, distress and corruption and the sheer size of the problems. We may become inured to so much information about so much suffering. Our sense of offence becomes blunted so that the Word may only become 'warm flesh' when the offence touches us immediately, in our own family, in our own town ....

William Blake's spirituality was often a spirituality of 'warm flesh', and offence was often raw and simple but social and political:

A Robin Redbreast in a cage
Puts all Heaven in a rage ...

... Nought can deform the human race
Like to the armourer's iron brace;
The soldier armed with sword and gun
Palsied strikes the summer's sun.
When gold and gems adorn the plough,
To peaceful arts shall Envy bow.
The beggar's rags fluttering in air
Do to rags the heavens tear;
The prince's robes and beggar's rags
Are toadstools on the miser's bags.

(from *Auguries of Innocence*)

Too often now our spirituality is disempowered, perhaps by the unbearable or inadmissible weight of human offence globally. So for some it becomes an ecclesiastical domain - spirituality done, as it were, on our behalf! For many, spirituality is highly individualised and privatised and yet, paradoxically, it is pre-packaged and sold to us. The commodification of religion in various ways is a mark of our consumer society. Here spirituality is offered to us by countless little books, courses and alternative therapies: what a Scottish minister (Ron Ferguson) has called, "the late-twentieth century's precious ego-spirituality". As an antidote he recommends *The Little Book of Complete Bollocks*:

> *Tired and sluggish? Make room in your life for your large intestine. Give it some attention. Ask it if it would be interested in colonic irrigation. Talk to your bottom about it. Listen to your bottom before taking a decision.*

As Ron Ferguson writes, this little book, parodying *The Little Book of Calm*, "hits the target of the soft, faery spirituality of our times" very effectively.

'LET MY BELOVED COME TO HIS GARDEN, AND EAT ITS CHOICEST FRUITS' (Song of Solomen 4:16)

We need a spirituality more vigorous: both more fleshly and more material. The Song of Solomon is a gloriously erotic poem. For me, at least, its spirituality lies within, essentially part of that erotic language, those erotic images in much the same way that some of D. H. Lawrence's prose and poetry is spiritual:

And when, throughout all the wild orgasms of love
slowly a gem forms, in the ancient, once-more-molten rocks
of two human hearts, two ancient rocks, a man's heart and a woman's,
that is the crystal of peace, the slow hard jewel of trust,
the sapphire of fidelity.

The gem of mutual peace emerging from the wild chaos
of love.
(from D. H. Lawrence, *Fidelity*)

The Word made warm flesh means more than that. It must mean the Word touching, suffering, healing, crying and rejoicing within each human situation, each person. For that to be real, it must mean the Word of God, of truth, love and justice working in, and shaping the structures of, those economic, political, religious and social realities within which people live. But religious people, Christians or others, do not have a monopoly on truth, love or justice; nor do they have a code of ethics and morality that provides right answers to each and every situation and problem.

It is true that religion, and certainly Judaeo-Christian scriptures, lay upon us some clear commands, invitations and challenges, some of which we see as universal requirements:

You have been told, man, what is good!
He requires only one thing from you:
do justice and be there for others,
match God in your life.
(Micah 6:8 transl. D. Solle)

'... and you shall love the Lord your God
with all your heart, and with all your soul,
and with all your mind, and with all your strength.'
The second [commandment] is this,
'You shall love your neighbour as yourself.'
There is no other commandment greater than these.
(Mark 12:29-31; also in Matthew and Luke)

But few if any of these ethical commands are situation specific. They are undoubtedly ethical requirements and responsibilities laid upon us, values, and ways of life and salvation whose meaning and application

we need to search out in each situation. They do not give us the answers, but they do, or they can, make us aware of the offence, make us aware of man's inhumanity to man - although the Catholic philosopher and theologian, Jacques Maritain (1882-1973), said we ought to give our thanks to Marx for showing us that.
So, making us aware, those ringing commands and challenges of love, justice, faithfulness, forgiveness, peace and reconciliation highlight the situation and the problem, and then leave us to search out their truth and meaning and application in a particular situation.
Perhaps the best image for that is the biblical story and Jacob Epstein's sculpture of Jacob wrestling with the angel. Again, it brings us back to warm, sweating, struggling flesh.

When Jacob and the angel had wrestled
until the break of day, the angel said,
"Your name shall no more be called Jacob, but Israel,
for you have striven with God and with men,
and have prevailed."
(For full context see Genesis 32:24-32)

We need to struggle, to wrestle with God and our fellow humans, for the Word to become warm flesh, for his Way, his Love, to course in the veins of our desires, our minds and our determination.

DANCING THE WORD

Konya, in Turkey, is the town where Mevlana Celaleddin Rumi lived (1207-73). He was the founder of the Whirling Dervishes. To European Christian ears that have only heard of Whirling Dervishes as some mad Muslim sect, Mevlana would not seem to be worth attending to - but we would be mistaken. Mevlana Rumi was a poet, scholar, mystic and philosopher and had apparently a very ecumenical turn of mind.

The mystical order of the Whirling Dervishes that he founded pointed to a deep and universal awareness. Their whirling dance was their worship and a recognition of the central truth of human life and possibility. As they whirled in their long, flowing robes, their right hands pointed upwards to heaven and their left hands downwards to earth. The dance illustrated the tension and possibility of the relationship between Heaven and Earth, God and Humankind.
Is that not another image of the Word of God?
Well might we wonder if Mevlana had read the Acts of St John in the Apocrypha:

Divine Grace is dancing: fain would I pipe for you.
Dance ye all!
All things join in the dance!
Ye who dance not, know not what we are knowing ...

Gustav Holst set that to music in his *Hymn to Jesus*, and T. S. Eliot reflects the same theme in 'Four Quartets' (Burnt Norton).

It arises again in Sydney Carter and the Shakers' song, 'Lord of the Dance'.
We are embodied people. Singing, wrestling, dancing, loving, doing, we are embodied people. We are not polarised people: mind/body, intellect/emotion, thought/imagination, all that is 'me' is embodied. Our bodies and our behaviour and our actions are carriers of all sorts of messages, are suffused with all sorts of values, drives, prejudices and assumptions. All of this is embodied - embodied in warm flesh. But so also the Word may be embodied in the warm flesh of the dancers, the wrestlers, the lovers, the doers ....
And no doubt the Word of God is alive and active within other religions, other creeds and cultures and histories. That is why some Christians would have found unacceptable, even offensive, a Christmas card that contained the words: 'Best Wishes for Christmas

and our Prayers that the New Year, New Century and New Millennium will see us and all the world owning Jesus Christ as our Lord.'
Is that not a Christian arrogance in this new century and new millennium when we live in an increasingly plural society and become increasingly aware of the plural nature of our Global Village? Especially when that awareness includes the recognition of the plurality of the domain of love and trust, goodness and faithfulness!
Part of the Word being made warm flesh must entail the coming to the warm flesh of different people, with different colours and cultures and histories and religions. God will surely not be confined by the accidents of our histories and colour and culture and religious tradition. Just as love and truth and justice, kindness and belonging are so much greater than any one people or place or creed, so is God.
As Robert Van de Weyer wrote in 1992:

> *For me the Decade of Evangelism is not primarily about persuading more bottoms on to the pews of my church, but about encouraging people to respond to the Word of God in every religion and in every aspect of life.*

A PARABLE

The Kingdom of God is like a young woman who devoted herself, body and soul, to the cello, coaxing from its cherished form a sound that captivated, thrilled and charmed the hearts and minds of millions. Jacqueline du Pres knew joy and sadness - emotions that even at the age of seventeen she was able to bring to her interpretation of Elgar's Cello Concerto with such discipline and authority that concert-goers and critics alike discovered afresh 'the inherent pathos of Elgar's melancholy masterpiece'.
Hers was a shy/confident, laughing/crying, spontaneous/disciplined cradling of her beloved cello so that, to watch her playing, she and the

cello were one; one instrument evoking from great music - revealing - 'glimpses of eternity'.
That is not the least changed, only is it both the more human and the more wonderful by knowing more now of the biographical details of her life.

APPENDIX

THE CASE OF BELIEFS AND HOMOSEXUALITY

What causes us to be homosexual? In fact we do not seem to know a great deal about the causes (the aetiology) of either heterosexuality or homosexuality. It is just accept as a natural fact - if you are heterosexual. But not so - if you are gay!

Given that social context, it is not surprising that gay people and communities are suspicious of the emphasis some place upon finding the 'causes' of homosexuality. They suspect that it is knowledge that will be used against them: 'If we knew the aetiology we could cure them'! But many gay men were aware of their difference from other boys, and even knew that they were gay, from the time they were eight or ten years of age. An increasing number of gay men and women are open about their sexual orientation and comfortable and happy with that.

To know the aetiology of homosexuality might be very helpful. It might be an affirmation of our gayness if, for example, the cause was shown to be genetic. (Time for an aside: some graffiti appeared on a hoarding, which read, 'My mother made me a homosexual!' Beside it someone had written, 'If I gave her the wool, would she make me one?') However, there seem to be at least six possible factors that may contribute to the aetiology of homosexuality - and indeed those same factors presumably contribute to the aetiology of heterosexuality: genetic, biological, psychological, emotional, social and cultural. No doubt there may be elements of learned behaviour and of social fashion and of what might be called dysfunctional relationships - and there is nothing new or specific to homosexuality about that!

Some solid knowledge would be welcomed by many gay people. But they would not see such knowledge as the 'justification' or 'permission' to be gay: that would be a 'straight' condescension, 'straight' arrogance. They do not need such justification or permission to be homosexual, any more than straight people need it to be heterosexual.

We are all embodied people, and we are all sexual people because that is part of our embodiment. Thus, our sexuality, whatever that is, is an essential part of our being. It cannot be separated from the rest of 'whatever makes me who I am'. Therefore our sexuality is carried into all our relationships, and our specifically sexual relationships are always more than just sexual acts. Our bodies and what we do with our bodies express, carry and are instinct with all sorts of emotions, thoughts, beliefs, culture and commitments, etc.

So intimate relationships between people involve much more than sex. Indeed, probably fundamental to any good, affectionate and affirming relationships is friendship. Friendship is not asexual. Sexual attraction is often present in friendship and friendship may include or exclude overt sexual behaviour. But in friendship we would expect such behaviour to be a part of an expression of that friendship and that it would be mutual, consensual, loving, caring, life-affirming and responsible with regard to possible consequences, be they pregnancy or transmission of some disease, or consequences to some other person. Some of us would go further and say that the full intimacy of sexual behaviour should only be within a stable, committed and long-term relationship - especially when children are involved.

Now, so far all we have said about relationships and friendships is that sex is equally relevant to gay and straight, heterosexual, homosexual and lesbian people. Gay people can live and enjoy full, loving, affirming and responsible relationships.

Why then do so many people and institutions react so strongly to the idea of gay relationships? Why does our society spurn, reject and vilify gay men and women? The answer cannot be because homosexuality is 'unnatural', 'against nature' or 'disordered': those claims don't stand up in the light of what has been noted so far.

An Esther Rantzen TV programme was about gay and lesbian people

and their experiences, pains, joys and failures of marriage. At one point a man in the studio audience objected to the use of the term 'gay' when, he stated, the correct word to use is 'catamite' (definition: a boy kept for homosexual purposes; sodomites' minion; from Greek, Ganymedes, cup-bearer to Zeus)!
There is the clue. The answer to that question is largely a matter of stigma and prejudice shrouded in ancient taboos that have nothing now to do with rationality - even if they ever had - and are carried across the centuries by religious belief.
The irrational prejudice is all the more clearly illustrated in terms of that particular interjection in the Esther Rantzen show by the fact that the gay men present and participating seriously and sensitively in discussion were mostly men in their late thirties, forties and over - by no means 'boys'!
The more common word, and probably the word that man had intended and the word that is so often used to vilify homosexual people, is 'sodomite'. To unravel that piece of homophobia we shall need to travel to the biblical town of Sodom.
The biblical story of Sodom and Gomorrah appears in the book of Genesis. So, let us turn to the Bible.

HOMOSEXUALITY AND THE BIBLE

When reading the Bible, we must be careful, as Tim Morrison pointed out, not to assume that the writers had our assumptions or worked with our value systems. Rather, we must allow it to speak from its own time to inform and reform our culture.
Most Christians still approach the Bible with essentially fundamentalist presuppositions, with a deep-seated instinct that the Bible is to be unquestioningly revered as the direct source of God's will and word, a single source of literal, inerrant truth. Thus, to weigh the authority of a text against its historical and cultural context, or to see it in the light of new social or scientific knowledge, will meet the

inevitable charge of 'getting round the plain meaning of scripture' or 'capitulating to the spirit of the age'.

Most dangerously of all, however, even personal conscience and ordinary human instincts of decency and justice will be suppressed if these appear to conflict with what is perceived as God's will revealed in Scripture. Jeffery John writes (see page 90):

> *The most acute problems for the would-be Bible-based Christian are raised by the New Testament's moral and social teaching, the area where modern semi-fundamentalism is most obviously selective.*

There are two closely comparable areas of Pauline theology: his teaching about homosexuality and his teaching about women.

In the second case, outside moral pressure has forced all to recognise that, at least, certain biblical teachings must sometimes be weighed against higher biblical principles and changed social conditions, and must sometimes be set aside.

However, that is not so with regard to the teaching about homosexuality. Indeed, rather the reverse: teaching, some of it unclear and uncertain, has been highlighted and strengthened by fears and prejudice - and not least the fears and ignorance about HIV and AIDS. For instance, read Genesis 18:16 to 19:11 (and also see a later parallel in Judges 19 especially vv. 16 to the end of the chapter), where the mob was bent upon a homosexual assault. But that does not mean that homosexuality or homosexual assault was the main element of this story, or was uppermost in the mind of the writer or in the minds of other biblical writers or, indeed, was for God the main sin of the people of Sodom.

It is nowhere said that Sodom was destroyed because of homosexual sin, as the following biblical texts illustrate:

1) (Genesis 18:20ff.) Sodom and Gomorrah were to be destroyed by God for their wickedness (unspecified). God had decided that

BEFORE the visit of the angels to Lot's house.

2) Old and New Testament references to the wickedness of Sodom do not specify the sin as homosexuality. For Ezekiel (16:48,49) "... not coming to the aid of the poor and needy" is the main wickedness of Sodom. For The Wisdom of Solomon (19:13,14), as apparently for Jesus (see Matthew 10:14,15; Luke 10:10-12), it is the wickedness of inhospitality!

The 'incidental' homosexual element of the Sodom story was only highlighted later (see the second century A.D. Epistle of Jude verse 7), and even there the wording is ambiguous and may mean, as in 2 Peter 2:7, the sexual (but not necessarily homosexual) 'licentiousness of the wicked' men of Sodom.
Even if we give more weight than seems to be justified to the sexual element of the story, it is not a story of homosexuality but of attempted gang-rape by the whole male population of the city (Genesis 19:4) and presumably most of those men were heterosexual! The attempt was the 'gang-rape' of two 'angels' (two male strangers) by the men of the city. In the Judges story the intention was the same, but the gang-rape carried out was in fact of the Levite's (the stranger's) concubine.
The word 'sodomite' or 'sodomy' does seem to arise from a misinterpretation of Genesis 18:20 in the light of Genesis 19:5 and the hyping up of the homosexual element of the story by the cultural and religious needs of later ages.
In Deuteronomy 23:17 and 1 Kings 14:24, the word 'sodomite' is now replaced by the more accurate words, 'cult prostitute'- whether male or female.

LEVITICUS 18:22 AND 20:13

These contain the only two direct prohibitions of homosexual acts in the Old Testament. However, we should note:

(a) Homosexual ACTS are condemned here, not homosexual orientation - there was no knowledge of any such category or orientation.

(b) Female homosexuality is not mentioned.

(c) It may be that the condemnation is linked to their belief at the time of the sanctity of semen (note the story of Onan in Genesis 38). Semen was believed to be, itself, the new life, the new person.

(d) The production of children had a high priority for Israel during the exile and resettlement periods. The book of Leviticus was composed shortly after the return from the Babylonian exile and the restoration of the Temple.

(e) These verses are part of the Holiness Code, a collection of mainly ritual regulations arising out of the exilic and immediate post-exilic period. Important to Israel was the need to distinguish themselves from the surrounding religions and cultures and to separate themselves from the 'impurities' of those religions and cultures.

The question for us is how authoritative is the Levitical prohibition for the Christian today?
Part of the answer may be through another question: why is it that those two verses alone are the only verses in the Holiness Code of the Old Testament (Leviticus chapters 17 to 26) to which any Christian moralists still continue to appeal?

1 CORINTHIANS 6:9,10

Here the problem is semantic. What do the Greek words used here and translated 'homosexuals' actually mean? What did they mean at the time they were written?

The confusion is obvious when you compare the many English translations used in different versions of the New Testament: homosexual, effeminate, sexual perverts, any who are guilty of unnatural crime, catamites or sodomites ....
It seems likely that the Greek words in question refer to homosexual practices observed in Gentile culture, notably, homosexual prostitution and also pederasty (homosexual acts between a man and a boy). There is no general condemnation of homosexuality.

1 TIMOTHY 1:9,10

Here again the argument turns upon the meaning of the Greek words translated as 'immoral persons', 'sodomites' and 'kidnappers'.
It is suggested that probably the author intends to list:

(i) illicit (hetero)sexual activity in general;
(ii) homosexual activity in general - but having in mind the particular practices of the surrounding pagan culture (homosexuality was seen by Judaism as a Gentile vice associated with idolatry); and
(iii) kidnapping and slave-dealing for whatever purposes.

ROMANS 1:24-27

It is important to see these verses in the context of chapters 1, 2 and 3. This is the only place in the Bible where we seem to find a theological argument against homosexual practice.
This Epistle is addressed to a Church composed of Jewish and Gentile converts. Paul's main interest here is not homosexuality but Gentile idolatry (see vv. 20-23) Then in chapter 2 he turns on the Jews. The condemnation is of both Gentile and Jew for "all have sinned and fall short of the glory of God" (3:23).
Note the word 'exchange' in 1:23,25,26. Here is the idea that "sexual

exchange reflects the primary exchange of the real God for idols. Disorder itself is not the primary sin but is rather the punishment of idolatry." Homosexuality itself is an example of a punishment that fits the crime of idolatry!

Paul portrays homosexuality as a perverse moral choice. His assumption, universal in Jewish writing on the subject, but not in Greek or Roman, was that homosexuality is freely chosen - in the same way that idolaters freely choose to suppress the truth about God - for what can be known about God is plain to them because God has shown it to them (Romans 1:19).

Paul believes that male and female homosexual activity is against nature, meaning not only against the created order but against their personal nature.

Note:

1) Paul assumes that homosexual activity is activity chosen by people who are naturally heterosexual. For him, it is an abandonment of 'normal' heterosexual relations. (Notice the parallel with idolatry!)

2) It is probable that Paul has in mind the two forms of homosexual activity present in Greco-Roman culture and abhorred by exilic and post-exilic Judaism: pederasty and prostitution.

It is unlikely that Paul was thinking of or could envisage the case of two adult men (or women) living together in a loving, stable and committed relationship!

GENESIS 1:26,27 AND 2:18

The weight given to these passages by biblical traditionalists is derived from Paul's basic presupposition that homosexual relationships, however seemingly moral and good, are in fact against

the God-given pattern of creation.
That pattern is exemplified for them by Genesis 1:27: "So God created man in his own image ..., male and female he created them." (That leads on to Matthew 19:4 and Mark 10:6 and to the Marriage Service.) As in the old 1662 Church of England Prayer Book, the first purpose of that relationship has for long been seen as, "First, it was ordained for the procreation of children ... ." But what was God's will in the creation of male and female? "Complementarity and companionship are at least as much a part of God's plan in creation as childbirth." In Genesis, childbirth is a secondary matter within the negative context of God's punishment of Eve (3:16), whereas in 2:18 it is NOT said, God created a companion for Adam for procreation, BUT because "It is not good that man should be alone"!

1 Corinthians 6:15-20; Ephesians 5, especially v.2

There is a fundamental teaching here about the sacramental character of human sexuality. Homosexual relationships are held by some to jettison that teaching because they are against 'natural law', against God's plan for creation, and are 'unnatural acts' wilfully chosen.
But if homosexuality IS NOT wilfully chosen but in fact is an indissoluble and inseparable part of the very being of a person, then a homosexual relationship may be capable of fulfilling every purpose of God in marriage, apart from childbirth.
Although Paul is speaking of heterosexual marriage, may it not also be that a homosexual relationship can reflect the same covenanted, creative, faithful and sacrificial love? The sacramental character of sexual relationships must depend more upon the quality of that relationship than upon the ability to procreate.
Rowan Williams, speaking about the significance of sexuality in the biblical tradition and commenting upon 1 Corinthians, said: "Sexual activity that does not symbolise, signify, speak of covenant faithfulness is a sham!"

My sexual life is meant to communicate God's covenant relationship with his created world, his people. "Sexuality is essentially a spiritual matter - about looking for Grace (the body's grace!)". In the Bible, marriage, love (see also Hosea) and sexuality (see the Song of Solomon) are seen as metaphors of God's covenant relationship and as illustrations of, and vocation to, faithful, committed, deep relationships reflective of God's love and faithfulness.

Numerous scholarly studies over the last 30 years conclude that "there is no solid ground at all in scripture from which to attack a loving and faithful relationship between two people of the same sex".

* * *

N.B. This section draws heavily upon the article written by the Revd Dr Jeffrey John, 'The Bible and Homosexuality', in *Christian Action Journal*, Summer 1990.

REFERENCES

SOME AUTHOR AND BOOKS REFERRED TO OR QUOTED

* Swami Abhishyiktananda: qu. in "Prayer of Hope of An Interfaith Man" by Daniel Faivre. BFSS Natonal RE cntre. ISBN: 1-87201201-9

* Author unknown: "The Cloud of Unknowing". Penhuin Classics.

* Stephen A. Cherry: "Running with the Foxes", articles in the Church Times, 7 October 2005.

* Richard Holloway: "Doubts and Loves - What is left Christianity". Canongate. ISBN: 1-84195-179-X

* Jelaluddin Rumi: "The Essential Rumi", translations by Coleman Barks. Castle Books. ISBN: 0-7858-0871-X

* Mary Doria Russell: "A Thread of Grace."

* Jonathan Sacks: "The Dignity of Difference." Continuum. ISBN: 0-8264-6850-0

* Jean-Francois Six: "Prayer & Hope." Collins, Fontana Library.

* Thomas L. Thompson: "The Bible in History - How writers create a past." Pimlico. ISBN: 0-7126-6748-2

* Desmond Tutu: "God Has a Dream - A Vision of Hope for our Time." Rider. ISBN: -844132-37-4. Reprinted by permission of The Random House Group Ltd.

* David Sloan Wilson: "Darwin's Cathedral - Evolution, Religion, and the Nature of Society." The Universaity of Chicago Press. ISBN: 0-226-90134-3

* Christopher Fry's Play: "A Sleep of Prisoners." Page 49 of the 1963 edition. By permission of Oxford University Press.

POEMS QUOTED:

* E. E. Cummings: Reprinted from "Complete Poems 1904-1962" Edited by George J. Firmage, by permission of W.W. Norton & Co. Copyright 1991 by the Trustees of the E. E. Cummings Trust and George James Firmage.

* Gerard Manley Hopkins: from "A selection of his poems and prose by W. H. Gardner." Penguin Books.

* D. H. Lawrence: "Fidelity" from DHL selected poems published by Penguin Books 1950. Reproduced by permission of Pollinger Limited and the proprietor.

* Robert Frost: from "In the Clearing." Page 101, 1962 Holt, Rinehart & Winston.

With thanks to authors and publishers and apologies if I have not managed to contact the appropriate source for permission - this will be corrected for future re-prints.